Also by Melissa Donovan

ADVENTURES IN WRITING (SERIES)

10 Core Practices for Better Writing
1200 Creative Writing Prompts

Adventures in Writing
101 Creative Writing Exercises

Adventures in Writing
101 Creative Writing Exercises
Melissa Donovan

Swan Hatch Press | San Francisco

ADVENTURES IN WRITING: 101 Creative Writing Exercises

Copyright © 2011 by Melissa Donovan

First Edition, 2012
Published by Swan Hatch Press • Melissa Donovan

ISBN 9780615547855

Table of Contents

Acknowledgments

I could not have written this book without the readers, subscribers, visitors, and commenters at Writing Forward who have inspired me and strengthened my dedication to writing and advocating for writers. I am eternally grateful to my mom for teaching me to read and write at a young age and instilling in me a passion for literature. I thank my dad for all of his support and encouragement.

Melissa Donovan

101 Creative Writing Exercises

Introduction

Writing is a way to communicate, but it is so much more than that. Through writing, we develop and share ideas and information. We express ourselves and make art.

Look around. The written word is everywhere. It's in books, movies, speeches, advertisements, and song lyrics. Writing is found on product packaging, computer monitors, smart-phone screens, greeting cards, and signs. Writing is all around us.

Writers are responsible for some of the greatest contributions to society and culture. We educate, entertain, sell, share, and make emotional connections.

The best writers make it look easy, as if the words roll onto the page with ease, but writing well requires tremendous effort. Our work demands concentration, patience, practice, and a willingness to experiment and take risks. Writers toil at the craft for years, building up an arsenal of tools, techniques, and skills.

Each writer comes to the craft for his or her own reasons. Some of us fell in love with magical tales and wondrous poems when we were children. Some of us are compelled to express our thoughts, opinions, and experiences. Some want to make art out of words. Some write for money. Some write for love.

There are a million reasons to write, and all of them are equally valid.

What You'll Find Inside This Book

The exercises in this book are designed to give you practical experience in writing across a range of forms and genres.

Some of these exercises provide tools and techniques that you can apply to your work. Other exercises inspire pragmatic writing projects that you may be able to submit for publication, such as stories, poetry, articles, and essays.

These exercises encourage you to explore the world of writing, help you build writing skills, and give you real-world experience and plenty of writing practice.

Exploring form, genre, style, and subject matter

Many writers are dedicated to one form or genre, and there's nothing wrong with that. This book is not going to try to convince a copywriter to become a poet or tell a novelist to start writing how-to manuals. But dabbling outside your favorite form or genre will strengthen your skills and equip you with effective methods and techniques that can be applied across all types of writing.

If you enjoy writing in different forms and genres, or if you haven't figured out what, exactly, you want to write, then these exercises will help you find your path.

Discovering tools and techniques (skill building)

You'll learn a lot by simply reading the exercises in this book. Each one includes a short introduction that presents literary terms, storytelling devices, and writing techniques that you can use in your own writing projects.

You'll learn about alliteration and assonance, the three-act story structure, and how to use metaphors and similes effectively. You'll experiment with writing by formula and writing in form. You'll also learn handy techniques that experienced and successful writers have been using for centuries, like discovery writing and outlining.

Creating fresh ideas and getting plenty of practice

Every exercise in this book is constructed so you'll learn something new about writing. These exercises are also designed to inspire you with fresh ideas for future writing projects. Many of the exercises in this book will help you develop projects that you can eventually polish, submit, and publish.

Through his research for the book *Outliers: The Story of Success*, Malcolm Gladwell established the 10,000-hour rule, which states that it takes ten thousand hours of practice to master any skill, craft, or trade. Many successful writers say you should never publish your first poem, short story, or novel. Instead, you should practice before you publish.

The exercises in this book give you plentitude and variety in your writing practice.

How to use this book

The exercises in this book are grouped by form, technique, and subject matter. One chapter focuses on poetry, while another emphasizes article writing. There's a chapter that looks closely at writing about people, both fictional and real, and another that promotes critical thinking.

You can work your way through the book from beginning to end, or you can choose exercises at random. You might select exercises that appeal to your mood, or you might choose chapters that address issues or problems you're having with your own writing projects.

You are encouraged, however, to step outside of your comfort zone. If you primarily write essays, then try a poetry exercise. You'll find that experimenting with one form of writing will reveal concepts and techniques that you can apply to another form. A blogger will learn a lot from doing storytelling exercises, and a fiction writer will learn how to better organize a story logically from the critical-thinking exercises.

Each exercise may include any or all of the following:

1. introduction of a writing concept

2. the steps or process for completing the exercise

3. tips to make the exercise easier or clearer

4. variations and alternatives to the exercise

5. practical applications that the exercise offers, including its role in publishable projects

Some of the exercises are more challenging than others. You might spend several writing sessions on one exercise and finish another in just a few minutes.

Use this book and work through the exercises in whatever way feels most comfortable to you. Please make sure you also challenge yourself. If one exercise sounds hard, push yourself to work through it. If another seems dull, use it as an opportunity to develop discipline.

You'll also find that you can do almost all of these exercises over and over again. Each time, they'll come out different.

Have fun and keep writing!

Chapter 1: Freewriting

Freewriting is one of the most creative and liberating writing exercises you can do.

Also called stream-of-consciousness writing, freewriting allows you to let your thoughts and ideas flow onto the page without inhibition. Anything goes. Turn off your inner editor and allow your subconscious to take over. The results can be inspiring, enlightening, and thought provoking.

Freewriting is ideal for daily writing practice. A twenty-minute freewriting session in the morning is an excellent way to capture your dreams or record your ideas before your head becomes cluttered with the day's activities. A nighttime session is perfect for clearing your mind of the day's clutter and for noting new ideas that have occurred to you throughout the day.

Guided freewriting is a bit different. As you write, you focus your attention on a specific idea, topic, or image. There are a number of variations on guided freewriting, which are explained in the variations section after the exercise.

With any kind of freewriting, you write quickly and let your thoughts flow freely. Remember, anything goes, even if it doesn't make sense. Thoughts that sound ridiculous as you're writing may gain meaning or clarity when you read it back later.

The Exercise

The process is simple. First, set a limit. Your limit is the minimum amount that you will write. Limits can be set in time, word count, or pages. Then write whatever comes to mind, no matter how outrageous. You will write up to your limit, and if you want, you can exceed it. In other words, if you set a limit of ten minutes, you must write for at least ten minutes, but you can write for longer if you want.

The first few times you try freewriting, you might find that your mind goes blank at different points in your writing session. When this happens, don't stop writing. Your pen should always be moving. If nothing comes to mind, write the word *nothing* over and over until your thoughts start flowing again. Just keep writing.

Tips: What limits should you set? If you have a timer, try setting it for twenty minutes, which is a good amount of time for any writing session. Or fill two pages in your notebook, writing in longhand. If you'll be writing electronically, then aim for five hundred words. You may want to experiment with how you set allotments for your freewriting sessions. Some writers find that anything beyond thirty minutes of freewriting becomes garbled; others find they hit their stride after the ten-minute mark.

Experiment with different writing tools. Many writers like writing in longhand for better creativity. If you write primarily on a computer, then give paper and pen a whirl for a few of your freewriting sessions.

Also, don't give up after your first attempt at freewriting. Most writers who are new to freewriting find that it takes a few tries to get the hang of it.

Variations: Below are a few examples of guided freewriting for creativity and problem solving:

Focused freewriting is writing around a certain idea or concept. If you're working on a novel, and your characters are stuck, a focused freewrite might help you break through the scene or move your characters to the next step. This is a bit like brainstorming, except you write freely and continuously, letting ideas stream instead of pondering them before committing them to the page.

Topical freewriting is writing about a specific topic or subject. If you're working on an essay, you might engage in focused freewriting about the subject matter. This allows you to explore your thoughts and feelings and figure out which ideas and aspects of the subject you want to examine or address.

Words and imagery freewriting is great for poetry writing and useful if you're writing *nothing* a lot in your general freewriting sessions. Choose a word or image and while you're freewriting, keep your mind focused on it. If your mind goes blank during the freewrite, come back to the word and write it over and over (instead of *nothing*). Some examples: *my body, apple tree, hummingbird, war, freedom, family,* or *library*.

Character freewriting helps you get to know your characters. There are two ways to do character freewrites. The first is to freewrite about the character. Write the character's name across the top of the page, set your timer, and then write whatever comes to mind about the character. The second method for character freewriting is to write in first person as if you are the character. This brings you inside your character's head to better understand his or her goals and motivations.

Solution freewriting is a technique for solving problems in your writing projects. Start by writing the problem across the top of the page. Try to form it into a question, and then write. Allow yourself to explore tangents and be emotional. You may find that you write yourself into a solution. Some examples include the following: *How can I explain the mystery I created for my story? What is missing from this poem? How can I better argue my position in this essay?*

Applications: Freewrites are perhaps best known for generating raw material that can be harvested for poetry. The nature of stream-of-consciousness writing lends itself well to poetry, because freewrites tend to produce unusual or vivid images and abstract ideas.

Freewrites are also perfect for daily writing practice, especially when you don't have a larger project underway or need a break from your regular writing routine.

Chapter 2: It's Personal

Personal essay, memoir, and journal writing exercises

2.1 Writer, Know Thyself

This exercise asks you to look in the mirror and ask yourself a critical question: Why do I write?

There are many forces that drive writers to the page. Some do it for love, for creative expression, or because writing is simply something they must do, a compulsion. Others do it for riches, for prestige, or to make a living.

It's not easy to succeed as a writer. Most writers have day jobs and write during their free time, chipping away at novels, drafting essays, articles, short stories, and poems. They spend their evenings polishing their work, and they spend their weekends submitting it to agents and editors. Some plan to self-publish. Many already have.

Writing professionally requires an immense amount of self-discipline, because in the early years, you're hustling. Trying to land gigs. Building up clips.

On top of self-discipline, writers are competing in a field that's saturated with dreamers and overrun with talent. Creativity is fleeting, gigs are scarce. Far too many novels end up half-finished and buried in a bottom drawer.

For those who intend to succeed, finish that novel, get that poem published, or earn a living wage as a freelance writer, staying focused is imperative.

Those who succeed are not the most talented or the smartest. They are the ones who refuse to give up. They have good writing habits; they are focused and motivated and consistently work toward their goals.

As a writer, it's important to know where you are in relation to your goals.

The Exercise

This exercise presents a series of questions about your goals and motivations as a writer. Your job is simple: Write a short paragraph to answer each question. Keep your answers concise and try not to go off on tangents.

You can revisit this exercise at least once a year to see how you're progressing, to stay focused and motivated, and to remember why you write.

If you are not ready to answer these questions, then set them aside and come back to them after you've worked through some of the other exercises in this book.

- What do you write, or what do you want to write? Think about form (fiction, poetry, memoir, etc.) and genre (literary, speculative, romance). Be specific.
- How often and how much do you write? Ask yourself whether you have enough time to write and whether you could make more time for your writing.
- What are your top three goals as a writer?
- Why are these three goals important to you?
- What is your five-year career plan as a writer? What do you need to do over the next five years to achieve one (or all) of your top three goals?
- In the past year, what have you accomplished in working toward your goals?

- What can you do over the next year to move closer to your top three goals and your five-year career plan?

Tips: Keep your goals separate and specific. If you want to publish a novel through legacy (traditional) publishing, you don't need an additional goal of getting an agent. Getting an agent is implied in the greater goal of legacy publishing.

If you have more than three goals, then list up to ten, but highlight your top three priorities.

If you're not sure what your goals are, then make goal-setting a goal. Give yourself some time to set goals (a few weeks or months).

Variations: Instead of answering all the questions in a single session, you can spread them out and answer one question a day. While concise answers will be the clearest, the first time you do this exercise, you might want to write a full-page response to each question. You can also use these questions as journal prompts and write your answers in your daily journal (see next exercise, "The 31-Day Journal").

Applications: These questions help you clarify your intentions. When you know what you want to accomplish, it becomes easier to attain. In addition, articulating your goals ensures that you can discuss them intelligibly, which comes in handy when submitting query letters, in meetings and interviews, and in discussions with other writers and professionals in the publishing industry.

2.2 The 31-Day Journal

Many journals follow a diary style for chronicling daily life, but a journal is also a space where a writer can explore ideas, work out problems, and reflect on themes and issues both real and imagined.

This exercise encourages you to try journal writing by experimenting with a few different types of journals. You can keep an idea journal for a week and then keep a reflective journal for a weekend. Or, rotate through the different types of journals for a few days each. Try all of them.

This is not only an exercise in exploring the many types of journals you can keep; it is also an exercise in discipline and building good writing habits through daily practice. As an added bonus, these journal-writing exercises also work as creativity boosters.

If you write for twenty minutes a day for thirty-one days, at the end of the month you will have developed a writing habit, and you will feel an impulse to write every single day. Try to keep your journal going past the thirty-one-day mark, but if you find that it doesn't benefit your writing or interest you, then move on and focus on daily writing through other exercises and writing practices.

The Exercise

Keep a daily journal for thirty-one days. Set aside a minimum of fifteen to twenty minutes each day for your journal-writing sessions. Over the course of the month, try each type of journal listed below. Make sure you try each one for at least a few days so you can truly get a feel for it.

Diary-Style: Diaries are recounts of the day's events. Some people keep diaries so they will remember their experiences later. Some hope their diary entries will eventually provide notes they can use in writing a memoir or autobiography. Many people keep diaries that they can pass along to their children, preserving their heritage. A few hope their diaries will become treasures for academics to sort through once they've made a literary mark by writing a prestigious novel or making a valuable contribution to society.

Diary writing helps you develop a daily writing habit. Keeping a diary also promotes memory and builds observation skills, which are essential for writers working in any field, form, or genre.

Self-Improvement: Nobody's completely satisfied with everything in life. There's always something else we want, whether it's a bigger salary, a smaller waistline, or the desire to write and publish a novel. A self-improvement journal is all about setting a single goal and then writing about your progress every day.

The fact that you're reading this book means that at the very least, you have some writing goals you'd like to achieve. You may want to find the form that's best for you, or perhaps you simply want to improve your writing skills. Pick any goal and write about your daily progress in a journal for a few days.

Reflective: Reflective journal writing falls somewhere between a diary and a personal essay. It weaves together a story from your life with your thoughts, beliefs, or lessons learned as they relate to that event.

Reflective journal writing goes beyond diary writing, because its intent is not to recount events but to put events into a context with deeper meaning.

Reflective journal writing requires that you pay attention to how you craft your sentences and paragraphs. You're telling a story and making thoughtful observations and conclusions about it. You are not limited to writing about the events of the day; you can reflect on any event or experience from your life.

Art Journal: Each day, try to experience some form of art or entertainment. Go to a museum and look at paintings and sculptures (or view them online). Listen to an album. Watch a foreign film. Try to experience a mixture of fine art and pop culture entertainment. Then, write about it.

Here are some questions to prompt your art journal entries: How did it make you feel? What did it inspire you to think about? How can one piece of art influence another? How do different mediums inform each other? How does what's happening in a culture inspire a novel or a poem?

Dream Journal: There's something mysterious and magical about dreams. In the dreamworld, anything is possible. Our deepest desires and greatest fears come to life. Whether they haunt or beguile, our dreams represent the far reaches of our imaginations.

Throughout history, dreams have often acted as catalysts for artists and inventors. You can use a dream as the foundation for a piece of writing. Your dreams can provide you with characters, scenes, imagery, and even plot ideas.

Keep a notebook by your bed for a few nights (or a few weeks, if necessary). As you're falling asleep, tell yourself that you will remember your dreams. As soon as you wake up, grab your journal and jot down everything you can remember.

Tips: Write in your journal at the same time every day. Wake up twenty minutes earlier so you can write, or take your journal to bed at night and do a twenty-minute session as a way to wind down from the day and get ready for sleep.

Variations: There are many more journals that you can keep. Some examples include gratitude journals, travel journals, and parenting journals. The idea is to write in your journal every day for thirty-one days and to write about yourself and your experiences.

Applications: There are two major benefits to keeping a journal. The first is daily writing practice, which is essential to any writer's development. Writing must become a habit, something you do as frequently and regularly as possible, regardless of how inspired you're feeling. Keeping a journal also promotes observation, self-awareness, and reflection, all skills that great writers must possess.

2.3 Making the Mundane Riveting

Every creative writer must learn to hold the reader's attention. There are many ways to do this. You can intrigue your readers with suspense or mystery. You can get them to become emotionally invested in characters. You can mesmerize them with dazzling language.

A true master can take something, anything, and make it interesting. In 1951, Ernest Hemingway published *The Old Man and the Sea*. Much of the story's narrative consists of an old man floating around in his boat, trying to catch a large marlin. Hemingway brought readers deep into the fisherman's life and turned what would, in most writers' hands, be a dull tale of description and introspection into a fascinating and gripping read.

Of course, what's riveting to you might make someone else fall asleep. A book that wins the Pulitzer Prize might bore you, whereas someone else thinks it's a rapturous work of art. Beauty has always been in the eye of the beholder, which is something to keep in mind as you tackle this exercise.

The Exercise

Take some event from your life and make it riveting. Tell it in a way that captivates readers. You can use an event that actually was exciting—an adventure or crazy experience you've had—to make the exercise a little easier. To truly challenge yourself, choose something relatively ordinary, such as a day at the office or a family holiday. Stick to the truth—in other words, don't fictionalize it. Write it as a story with a beginning, middle, and end. Aim for about fifteen hundred words and write it in first person (from your perspective).

Tips: Many students are given the following assignment: write about a memory from your childhood. Their papers are often boring recounts: *One year my family went to Disneyland. The plane ride was scary, but the rides were fun. We stayed in a big hotel.* That's boring! Think about how the story unfolds for the reader. Think about word choice: *My childhood dream was to visit*

Disneyland, but I thought it would never happen. We didn't have much money. So when my parents loaded us into the car and said we were going on vacation, I figured it was another trip to my grandparents' house—until we pulled into the airport.

Variations: Write your story in third-person narrative.

Applications: Many literary journals and magazines accept personal essays. Many others accept short stories. This exercise has the potential to turn into a piece that you could submit for publication. It could also act as the foundation for a memoir, which is a focused narrative about an author's real-life experience.

2.4 Show Some Appreciation (or Emotion)

One of the most popular forms of personal writing is a gratitude journal. These journals are hailed for helping people maintain a positive attitude and stay focused on what matters.

Writers have to face extraordinary challenges that many other professionals never have to deal with: working for free to build skills and gain experience, piles of rejection slips, and the hassle of writing query letters and sending submissions. Most other professionals merely send a resume and cover letter and then go for an interview.

It's easy to get discouraged and stressed out. When life as a writer brings you down, gratitude can lift you up.

However, this exercise has other benefits. Are you prone to writing dark or sad poems or stories? Many young writers say the only thing that inspires them is heartache. Appreciation writing teaches you to write about joy, too. This comes in handy whether you're writing a self-help article for a magazine or creating a character with a positive attitude.

The Exercise

Start by writing a list of all the things in life for which you're grateful. These can be big things like family, home, and food, or little things like your favorite book, a sunny day, or a stranger's smile. Your list should have at least twenty-five items on it, but feel free to write as many as you can think of. When you're done, choose one item and write a short piece (500–750 words) about it. Try to answer all of the following questions:

- What am I grateful for?

- How does it make my life better?

- What would my life be like without it?

- How do I show my appreciation?

When you're done, reread the piece and polish it. Whenever you're feeling down, revisit the piece you wrote, or do this exercise again for a lift.

Tips: You can include appreciation-journal writing in your existing journal. Just write a short list of things you're grateful for every morning when you wake up. This starts your day on a positive note. You can also keep a journal that is strictly for gratitude. Instead of listing what you're grateful for, write a little bit each day about one thing that makes you feel appreciative.

Variations: This exercise is not limited to gratitude. In fact, you can tweak it for any emotion imaginable. You can write about things that make you mad, sad, confused, excited, hopeful, or inspired. Whatever emotion you choose, try to select words that are infused with that emotion. When writing about gratitude, use positive language and avoid negative words.

Applications: Writing is a great way to explore your emotions. Experience will teach you to write in a way that is emotionally appealing to an audience. When readers connect emotionally to something you've written, you've hooked them. Learning to deal with emotion in your writing is therefore an extremely valuable skill that can be applied across all forms of writing.

2.5 Your Bare Essentials

You can take a story or an event and strip it down to its most basic elements in order to examine its core ideas and subject matter. There are a number of techniques that you can use to accomplish this: lists, outlines, mind maps, and storyboards.

Sometimes our writing goes off on tangents. It wanders away from the core subject matter or theme. If we sit down to write a persuasive essay on the health benefits of drinking plenty of water, we might wander off into a tirade on the unhealthy quality of soda pop. In a story, we might follow a supporting character into a tangential series of actions that are loosely relevant, but not essential, to the plot.

The best writing stays focused on a core idea or message. If we use discovery writing (writing without a plan), we may realize ideas we otherwise wouldn't have imagined. On the other hand, we might find ourselves straying from the heart of what we're writing. Learning to stay on message takes practice and planning.

The Exercise

Choose a real-life experience you've had, and pare it down to its core elements by writing an outline.

Here are some suggestions: your earliest memory, most embarrassing moment, an ordinary day in your life, a vacation, adventure, losing a loved one, or falling in love.

Choose something concrete, and make sure it's something you remember well.

Write an outline detailing your event. In a sense, you're creating a timeline. Start by making a list of everything that happened. If you're writing about a vacation, the first item on the list would be when you initially had the notion to take that vacation. The second item would be when you bought tickets and reserved a hotel room. The third item might be packing.

Then review your list and add anything you might have left out. If you're listing a sequence of events related to a vacation, you might recall a conversation you had with someone who had taken a similar trip. Add it to the list.

Finally, go through your list again and highlight the most interesting events and actions, the ones that would warrant inclusion in an essay or story about your experience.

Tips: Use roman numerals (I, II, III) to list the main ideas or actions. Use capital letters for supporting ideas and numbers for details. Here's an example:

I. Made Reservations

    A. Airline tickets

B. Hotel reservations

    1. Hotel offers rental cars and free shuttle service

Variations: Draw a mind map. Write the core event in the middle of a piece of paper and draw a circle or box around it. Then write all the related actions and events around that bubble, and connect them to the main idea with lines.

Applications: Outlining streamlines the writing process. If you plan ahead, then you will spend less time revising. Many writers simply start writing about that vacation. Once the piece is complete, they might realize they left out a whole day or some funny thing that happened. You don't have to outline everything you write, but an outline often minimizes the number of revisions required in order to polish and fine-tune a piece.

You can use the outline you created to write a story or essay. Focus on making it engaging and entertaining.

2.6 Silver Lining

This exercise encourages you to think about lessons and messages in your writing. These shouldn't be obvious. In fact, stories that blatantly build up to a lesson or I-told-you-so moment usually fall flat with readers, because they come across as preachy or dogmatic.

Lessons and messages work best when they are subtle. Readers want to use their minds, so make them think about what the underlying themes of the piece are.

On a more personal level, this exercise asks you to look at your own life experiences in a new way. This thinking exercise challenges you to reevaluate cause and effect.

The Exercise

Think about an event in your life that was unpleasant. It could be the loss of a loved one, your first heartbreak, an illness, or any other trauma or malady. It can be something serious or a minor disappointment. It has to be something that, at the time, was a negative experience.

Your challenge is to find the silver lining. What good came out of your terrible experience?

Keep in mind that most negative experiences carry great lessons. They are also links in the chain of life that, if broken, may change or affect everything that has happened since.

Tips: Write about the painful event and transition into its silver lining without being obvious about it. Focus on telling your story as somewhat of a tragedy. Avoid hinting at the good that came from it until it actually comes. Or focus on the silver lining, and use flashbacks to demonstrate that the joys of today are built on the pains of yesterday.

Variations: Instead of finding the silver lining in a negative experience, write about something bad that came out of something that initially appeared to be a blessing.

Applications: Lessons and silver linings are almost always woven through stories, fictional and true. Understanding chains of events and how the balance of good and bad experiences shapes our lives is essential to good writing. You can use this exercise to write a personal story or essay in the style of a memoir that you can submit or publish.

2.7 Report It

Is your life newsworthy? Have you ever witnessed, committed, or been the victim of a crime? Have you ever participated in a protest or a performance? Have you ever had an odd or unusual experience?

Traditionally, professional journalism adheres to a set of ethics, focusing on the facts and details of the story and presenting those facts thoroughly and objectively. The traditional journalist does not inject his or her feelings or opinions. Journalists and reporters inform readers by revealing the who, what, where, when, why, and how of a news story.

Journalists are human. The news media in general is increasingly accused of using a variety of creative tactics to spin the news in favor of its own religious, political, or financial agendas. For example, in a report, a journalist should not badmouth a suspected criminal, but that journalist can include a quote from a witness who has badmouthed the criminal while intentionally not including a positive quote from some other witness.

Journalists can pick and choose quotes, facts, and even which stories to report.

Journalists and reporters are responsible for feeding us information about what's going on in the world. Yet considering that they are mere human beings, flawed, emotional, and opinionated just like the rest of us, one can only begin to imagine how spun the news actually is.

The Exercise

Revisit your past and write a news report about something you experienced firsthand.

The rules are simple: straight journalism. Refrain from including your personal feelings or opinions and don't take sides.

Write about the event as if you are a reporter looking in on your life from the outside. Answer these six questions: who was involved, what happened, where did it happen, when did it happen, how did it happen, and why did it happen?

Make sure you include a headline that will attract readers.

Tips: To get a feeling for how journalism is written (its tone and style), visit a reputable news site and read a few articles. As you do this, keep an eye out for reports and articles that are infused with the journalists' opinions or personal views. How easy are they to spot?

Variations: Instead of reporting a story, write a gossip piece: Were you spotted while out on a hot date? If you're at a loss for subject matter, get creative and write a fictional news story; make something up, change something from your past, or better yet, write a news story from your future (maybe you win the Pulitzer Prize in ten years).

Applications: The most obvious application is that you could, someday, become a journalist or a reporter. Journalism is an objective style of writing (at least, it's supposed to be). This exercise encourages you to write about something you care about while refraining from including your feelings or personal views.

2.8 Reader Response

There is nothing that will teach you more about writing than reading. Although books on the craft of writing are extremely helpful, reading novels, poetry, memoirs, and other published works regularly and frequently will enhance your writing skills faster and more fully than anything else you can do.

Reading will strengthen your writing; taking time to generate a thoughtful response to what you've read will strengthen it even more. Every writer should keep a reading journal. It's a place to note and explore thoughtful responses to what you've read and will help you gain a deeper understanding of your reading material. This kind of insight is invaluable for a writer.

The very act of writing promotes critical thinking. When we write, we are forced to clarify our thoughts. Often, through this process, our ideas crystallize. We may realize something about a story we've read that was not immediately obvious, but upon reflection, becomes integral to helping us understand it.

This deeper level of understanding benefits our own writing immensely, which is why writing critically about material we read is one of the best practices for building comprehensive writing skills.

The Exercise

Write a reader response to a single piece that you've read. This exercise will be more beneficial if you explore a full-length book: a novel, a memoir, or a collection of poems or essays. If you're strapped for time, you can choose a short story or a single poem or essay. Don't retell the story; just share your reaction to it. You are encouraged to build on this exercise and make a habit of thinking critically about your reading material by keeping a reading journal.

Tips: Here are some questions and prompts to get you started:

1. How did the book make you feel? Were you sad? Scared? Intrigued?
2. What was it about the story that evoked an emotional response from you? The characters? The plot? The subtext or themes?
3. Did you feel more like an observer, or were you pulled into the story, more like a participant?
4. How did the author build tension? Write down each pinnacle or event that led to the final climax.
5. Was it a page-turner? What were the hooks or cliffhangers that made you want to keep reading?
6. What was uniquely likable about the protagonist? What made the antagonist bothersome or despicable?
7. How would you describe the tone of the narrative? Was the prose flowery or poetic? Vulnerable or stoic?
8. Did the cover and title make you want to read the piece? How do they represent the book and compel readers?
9. How was the book structured? Did it have chapters? Were they numbered or named? Was there an introduction, prologue, or epilogue? A table of contents? To whom was the book dedicated? Who is the publisher? Whom did the author thank in the acknowledgments?

Variations: You can also apply this exercise to a film, album, or art collection. View the work with a writer's eye and compose your response as both an analyst (so you can cull writing techniques from it) and as a reader or member of an audience.

Applications: A good story analysis and response can be repurposed into a book review or an essay that deconstructs the work. There are plenty of literary journals and blogs that accept submissions of this nature.

2.9 Reflections

A memoir is a book-length autobiographical narrative that is almost always written in first person. Unlike a regular autobiography, a memoir is not a life story. It revolves around a particular theme, idea, event, or experience.

Memoirs are similar to personal essays or reflective writing. However, memoirs tell a story. A memoir may contain a message or lesson, but this is not mandatory.

Memoirs often take a reader inside unique lifestyles or experiences. Examples include being a prisoner of war, coping with illness, and achieving personal or professional success; there are also adventure or travel memoirs. Stephen King's book *On Writing* features a memoir about King's journey to becoming a wildly successful author followed by his recommended writing techniques.

The Exercise

Think about an experience you've had or an aspect of your life that readers might find interesting. Perhaps you spent a year living in another country. Maybe you held an unusual job or had some other unique experience.

Instead of writing a full memoir (that would be quite a feat for one writing exercise), write a synopsis for your memoir.

A synopsis is a summary of the book designed to interest readers. A synopsis doesn't give away the ending; it highlights key elements within the narrative.

Tips: Don't stray from the theme. If your memoir is about your life as a dog walker, leave out the story about the time you fell off the slide and had to have fifteen stitches (unless, of course, this event is somehow tied directly to your life as a dog walker). Using questions in a synopsis can be effective: *Ever considered your own dog-walking business?* To prepare for this exercise, read the synopses of a few memoirs (check the back covers).

Variations: If you're inclined, go ahead and write your memoir, or write the first chapter and see if it works as a personal essay. If you're struggling to come up with a concept for your memoir, you can instead write a synopsis for a memoir you've recently read.

Applications: This writing exercise is good practice if you intend to write a book someday. If you plan to take the traditional publishing route, you'll have to write synopses for agents and editors and try to convince them to read the rest of your manuscript. If you self-publish, then your synopsis will be one of your most important marketing tools. This exercise also encourages you to think about a broad topic (your life) through the lens of a single theme.

2.10 Your Author's Bio

If you ever get your own website or blog or publish a book, article, or pretty much anything else, you will have to write your author's bio.

You should know ahead of time that almost all writers despise writing their own bios, but it's something that has to be done. For published authors, a bio is especially essential, because it will be used as part of your press kit. Whenever someone reviews your work or interviews you, they're going to look at your bio to get some basic information. Your most loyal fans will also want to read your bio to get to know you better.

Why do authors find this process so tedious? Well, we have led full and complex lives. A bio asks us to distill our life into a page (or less). If you have tons of writing credits, you might be forced to squeeze some out. If you don't have any, you'll be pressed to fill out your bio adequately.

Of course, one of the best ways to get ideas for how to construct your bio is to visit other authors' websites to see how they've composed their own bios.

Many bios will briefly mention the writer's other hobbies or interests, but these should be kept to a minimum. A bio should focus on who you are *as a writer*. However, the last paragraph or sentence of a bio often states where the author lives and whom he or she lives with (spouse, children, pets).

The Exercise

Spend some time looking at professional authors' bios, and then write your own. It should be approximately 250–350 words, written in third person, and it should focus on who you are as a writer. Take your time and go over your bio several times, editing and polishing it.

Tips: Try to make your bio as clear and concise as possible. Would you send this to a newspaper or magazine? If not, keep working on it.

Variations: Write a 140-character bio for Twitter (this should be in first person). Try writing a short fifty-word bio (about the length that appears in article bylines and "About the Author" boxes on blogs and in newspapers).

Applications: You can use your bio on your blog or website. You'll also find that you can extract excerpts from your bio to fill out profiles on various social media websites, especially once you get active with marketing and promoting yourself as a writer.

Chapter 3: People and Characters

Individuals and group dynamics

3.1 People Are People

People and characters are among the most important elements in a piece of writing. In nonfiction, you need to treat subjects fairly, and in fiction, you need to make your characters believable.

To create the effect that a character, a made-up person, is real, a writer must have a deep understanding of people. What motivates them? What are their fears? What are their strengths and weaknesses?

Writing about real people presents its own set of challenges. If you're writing about someone whom you adore or respect, how do you deal with their flaws, mistakes, and weaknesses? If you are writing about someone you despise, how do you treat them fairly or objectively?

When you're telling someone else's story, you take on a huge responsibility. Whether the people you write about are real or imagined, it's a tough job.

The Exercise

Choose a real person and write a short story from that person's life. This piece will be nonfiction, written in third person. Your mission is to tell a story rather than write a biographical piece. Use the prompts below if you need ideas:

1. Some relationships are complicated: siblings who don't speak to each other, couples who sleep in separate rooms, exes who still come to holiday dinners.

2. Choose a celebrity or historical figure to write about. It can be someone living or dead. Do a little research about the person and then write a short piece telling a part of his or her story.

3. There's always a bad apple in the barrel: the bully on the playground, the snitch in the office, and the drama queen who stirs up trouble at every opportunity. They have stories, too!

4. Authority figures: parents, bosses, and government officials. You know them; they're in charge of the world. What's their story?

5. Bonus: for this prompt, you get to mix in a little fiction. Everybody loves a mysterious stranger. The cute barista. The handsome doctor. The eccentric woman who sits on the park bench every Thursday afternoon. Think of an interesting stranger you've seen around and concoct his or her story.

Tips: To add realism to your story, use dialogue, mannerisms, and gestures. Don't spend too much time on physical descriptions; a few, choice details will suffice. Focus on revealing the inner conflict and struggles of your subjects through their words and actions.

Variations: Instead of writing a nonfiction piece, write fiction, but use a real person as inspiration for your main character.

Applications: If you can tell a good story about someone, you can probably get it published, whether it's fiction or not.

3.2 We Are Family

They say you can pick your nose and you can pick your friends, but you can't pick your family. In this exercise, you can pick anyone you want, but it has to be someone you know personally.

As a writer, you will find that you are occasionally called upon for obligatory writing duties. A friend might ask you to proofread her wedding announcement. Your mother might ask you to write your grandfather's obituary. Requests for birth announcements, speeches, and eulogies may land on your doorstep with astounding frequency. After all, you're the token writer among your friends, family, and coworkers.

This exercise will teach you how to write a piece that is personal and emotional while also respectful and somewhat formal.

The Exercise

Draw upon your inner circle of family and friends, and write one of the following:

- birth announcement
- obituary or eulogy
- wedding announcement, or best-man or maid-of-honor speech
- graduation (or valedictorian) speech
- retirement speech

Tips: Consider your tone carefully. An obituary or wedding announcement is formal and respectful. Eulogies and wedding speeches can be tender or humorous.

Variations: Write a news profile, such as one you'd see if someone was running for office and was profiled in a local newspaper.

Applications: Writing pieces with this level of importance can be intimidating. For example, writing a speech that you'll have to deliver might be so terrifying that you just can't think of anything appropriate to write. Writing an obituary or eulogy for a loved one can be painful. These are important documentations of our lives and our loved ones' lives, and writing these pieces is an honor. This exercise gives you practice writing in a private but formal manner and also gives you experience in dealing with emotional subject matter.

3.3 Biography

Often, in studying another person closely and listing their most significant accomplishments and life events, we gain a deeper understanding of them.

We can learn a lot from other people. We study the lives of great leaders, celebrated artists, and innovators who have contributed to our cultures in meaningful ways. Put simply, the biggest human interest is other humans.

A biography is nothing more than all the facts about a person's life arranged into sentences and paragraphs that are organized and interesting. It sounds easy enough, but you'll find that there are hurdles to overcome in biography writing.

For example, do you humanize a serial killer by mentioning his beloved childhood pet or the charity work he did in college? Do you include your favorite politician's extramarital affair from thirty years ago? Which facts are objective and relevant?

In a well-written bio, facts are not overlooked or selected to give the subject a slant of the author's choosing. A good biography is honest and objective. However, in reality, biographies are often biased (or spun). If you were on a politician's campaign, for example, you'd write a spin piece and leave out all the negative information. But if you were on the opponent's campaign, you'd probably spin it the other way and make it all negative. And if you were an objective journalist, you'd simply look for the truth.

In a short bio, you can't include every detail. You're going to have to choose which facts from the subject's life are relevant.

The Exercise

Most biographies are about famous people. However, there are already enough of those biographies occupying shelves in libraries and the servers that hold Wikipedia. In this exercise, you'll write a biography of someone you know.

You can use a fake name, but you have to stick to the facts. Before you start, decide whether you'll do a spin piece or an objective piece.

Tips: Identify your target audience and a publication for the piece. This will help you narrow your focus. For example, you might write a bio about your mom in the context that she is running for president. You might write a piece profiling your best friend as a local small-business owner. You could also write a Wikipedia-style article about anyone you know, but try to emphasize their greatest achievements (good or bad) to justify their presence in an encyclopedia.

Variations: If you're up to the task, write one spin piece and one objective piece. Write both about the same person. As another alternative, write a detailed outline for a book-length biography about someone you know.

Applications: This exercise comes in handy if you ever write an article or essay about a famous or historical figure, or if you ever need to write your own biography. It's also a great starting place for coming up with characters.

3.4 *Character Sketch*

Creating characters is one of the most exhilarating exercises that a writer can work through. You get to make a person! And you can make that person out of nothing, you can base the character on someone you know, or you can combine ideas from your imagination with traits and qualities of real people.

If you write fiction long enough, you'll find that some characters arrive fully formed in your mind. Others are shy; they take a while to get to know. You know their names but can't picture their faces. You know their professions but can't put a finger on their goals. Their strengths are obvious, but surely they have weaknesses too!

Yet the biggest challenge in creating a character is making the character realistic. Your reader has to believe this character is a living, breathing person, even though he or she is just a figment of your imagination. If you can create a believable character, you're a skilled writer indeed.

The Exercise

A character sketch is a lot like a bio except the person is made-up, not real. For this exercise, you'll write a bio for a person you've invented. Here are some bits of information that you should include:

1. Name and physical description: What does your character look like? How does he or she dress? Try to come up with one unique identifying feature, like a mole or birthmark, a twitch or limp, freckles or bitten fingernails.

2. Family background: Where did your character grow up? What were the character's parents like? Don't go into too much detail about your character's family but feel free to include a few simple details.

3. Education and career: Is your character educated? Intelligent? What does he or she do for a living? How many jobs has your character held?

4. Significant relationships: Is your character married? A parent? Who are the important people in your character's life?

5. Personality traits: Is your character moody or laid back? Shy or outgoing? Passive or aggressive? How does your character behave in public? In private? What are your character's goals and motivations? Strengths? Weaknesses?

6. General history: What significant experiences has your character had? These could be anything from a traumatic event in childhood to losing a loved one as a young adult.

Tips: If you think you might use this character in a piece of fiction, then write the sketch right up to the point in your character's life when the story starts. For example, if your story features a character who is thirty-two years old, then your character sketch should cover the first thirty-one years of your character's life. Remember, a sketch is all about the highlights—don't write the story; just sketch the character.

Variations: For an extra challenge, write a sketch for a character who is nonhuman or create a cast of characters.

Applications: Character sketches are great warm-ups for writing short stories and full-length novels. You can also use your character in a fictional role-playing game.

3.5 The Bad Guy

Some writers excel at crafting villains. Others struggle because villains have to do cruel things to the other characters. Villains are mean. If you're a good person, you might find it hard to get into the mind of someone who is unsavory or downright evil. If you want to write good fiction, you have to be able to wiggle into a lot of different minds, many of which bear no resemblance to your own.

There are several types of villains. Lord Voldemort from the *Harry Potter* series is an absolute villain who is truly and totally evil. You never see him doing anything nice.

There are also sympathetic villains who are a little more human. Yeah, they're bad guys, lowlifes, or jerks, but they also have redeeming qualities. Hannibal Lecter from *Silence of the Lambs* was a psychopath, but he never hurt Clarice. He must have had some good in him, right? These villains tend to be a little more believable and a lot more sympathetic, because absolute villains are actually pretty rare in real life, if they exist at all.

Another type of villain is the uncertain or perceived villain. These are characters who appear to be threatening to a protagonist (the hero or main character in a story), but we're not sure about their true nature. They are classic *others*, characters who are perceived as enemies because they are the ones causing conflict. However, we don't know their motives or whether they are good or evil. Sometimes they're both or neither.

In fiction, an antagonist doesn't have to be a villain at all. The character who provides a source of conflict for the protagonist can be good, evil, or neutral. For this exercise, we'll focus on the evil variety of antagonists.

The Exercise

Write a short scene in which a protagonist first meets or learns about a villain.

Tips: In some stories, the moment when the protagonist and antagonist meet is climactic. In other stories, the antagonist isn't apparent as an opposing force until the story unfolds. Before starting this exercise, think about some of your favorite stories and recall the hero's interactions with the villain. The best insight into storytelling often comes from simple observation.

Variations: Try doing a character sketch for a villain (see exercise 3.4).

Applications: Every story needs an antagonist, and villains are always up to the task of antagonizing a hero. If you decide to write a short story or a novel, you can use the villain you've created and the scene you've written.

3.6 Getting into Character

In fiction writing, authors are like actors. While writers don't physically act out every scene, they certainly play the scenes out in their minds. To do this, a writer has to get into the characters' heads, just like actors do.

Unlike an actor, a writer doesn't have the leisure of occupying a single character for the duration of a story. A writer must be all of the characters, all of the time.

One minute you're in the mind of a gang leader, and the next minute, you're in the mind of a small child. A few minutes later, you're a bartender, and then you're a bum. While these constant shifts can be exciting, they are also challenging.

The good news is that it gets easier with practice. Start slowly, with one or two characters. Once you get the hang of it, you can bring more characters into the fold. This exercise is a good starting place, because it forces you to become someone other than yourself for a few pages.

The Exercise

You can use a character you've already created, or you can create a new one. You can also become someone you know from real life or choose someone famous. Your job is to write a two-page monologue in the character's voice (first person).

Before you start the exercise, make sure your character or subject has something to say. He or she should be talking about something specific, preferably something dramatic. A great approach is to have the character either relate a story from personal experience or reflect on his or her thoughts and feelings about a significant event.

Tips: You might want to do a little research to help you get into your character's mind. For example, if you've chosen a celebrity, you can watch interviews to see how he or she behaves and thinks.

Try to capture the voice of your character. The most vivid characters can be identified through distinct dialogue (phrasings and figures of speech), physical mannerisms, and gestures.

Watch out for filler words and phrases. Since the character is speaking, the audience knows whatever the character says represents his or her thoughts, feelings, and beliefs. Avoid phrases like *I think, I feel, I believe,* or *I wonder.*

Variations: As an alternative to writing a monologue, write a few diary-style journal entries as your character.

Applications: Monologues are quite common in plays and films. They also appear in stories and can be turned into pieces of performance art.

3.7 Character Study

Nobody's perfect, but in fiction, we tend to idealize characters. Have you ever noticed that lots of heroes always do the right thing? Villains will be mean just for the sake of being mean, even when they don't gain anything by it.

The same thing happens in nonfiction writing. Often, an article or biography has a specific purpose—to promote or smear someone. Just read any political article or glance at a gossip rag, and you'll see that most writers overtly fawn or frown upon their subjects.

The most interesting pieces of writing give us characters and people who are complex. They have respectable attributes, but sometimes they make mistakes. They have secrets. Under the right circumstances, they will take the heroic route. On a bad day, they could easily take the villainous path.

One of the best ways to learn how to create a realistic character is to study great characters from your favorite stories and interesting people from the real world. Observe their actions, choices, and words.

The Exercise

First, you'll need to choose a character from a story that you're well acquainted with. You can choose a character from a movie, television show, or book that you know intimately. If you need to watch or read again, do so (this is why a movie might be the best choice for this exercise—you can watch it and then do the exercise, whereas it will take you longer to watch a TV series or read a novel). Choose a character who is interesting, puzzling, or mysterious. The more complex, the better.

Your job is to write a character study. A study is different from a sketch because you're examining a character, whereas in a sketch, you're creating a character. It's different from a bio, because you're not merely highlighting significant events and accomplishments in the character's life. You're goal is to get inside the character's head.

Start by listing the basic facts: name, age, physical description, occupation, etc. Then dig deeper and ask some probing questions about the character you've chosen:

1. When the character makes a choice, what are his or her prime motivations behind that particular decision?

2. What mistakes has the character made?

3. What are the character's secrets?

4. Look for moments where the character's words or actions could be interpreted in more than one way.

5. You may view the character one way, and the other characters may have their own perceptions of the character, but how does this character see himself or herself?

6. What significant events shaped the character's personality?

7. Where are the character's loyalties? Why does the character possess these particular loyalties?

8. How does one action or decision that the character makes set off a chain of events?

9. Think about the character in terms of mind, heart, and spirit. What makes this character tick?

Tips: Look for subtleties. In a way, you are psychoanalyzing this character. Even a top-notch psychiatrist will not know every aspect of a patient's mind and heart. Often, the greatest insight we gain into people (real or made-up) happens in minor moments that could just as easily go unnoticed.

Variations: Try this exercise with a real person instead of with a character.

Applications: There is no better way to learn about people and characters than by simply studying them. This exercise helps you develop a writer's eye for how you view people in real life and characters in existing stories. Continue to look closely at characters and people. Think about the things they say and do, and ask why they are the way they are.

3.8 Nothing is Absolute

Story elements are often absolute. The villain is 100 percent evil; the protagonist and his or her friends are pure, good, and innocent. The world is dystopian or utopian. It's the best day ever or the worst day ever.

A lot of writers lean to extremes and polarities, which can make a story more exciting and dramatic. In some cases, absolutes make a story more effective. For example, it's a lot easier to blow up the enemy camp when you believe everyone in it is evil.

However, absolutes in stories are unrealistic. Readers actually become a lot more emotionally invested in a villain who is potentially redeemable. The reason for this is simple: we're all fallible, we've all made mistakes, and we're all imperfect. Redeemable villains and heroes who make bad choices appeal to us because see ourselves in them. And we want to believe that we can be redeemed, too.

The Exercise

The most popular science fiction, fantasy, and superhero stories feature absolute villains and heroes.

Find five heroes and five villains who are not absolutely good or evil. They can be real people from history or current events, or they can be characters from fiction (TV, movies, and books). For each one, write a short paragraph describing his or her good side and another short paragraph describing his or her bad side.

Tips: Choose a mix of characters, including supporting characters and sidekicks. Are main characters more or less likely to be absolutely good or evil?

Variations: You can turn this exercise on its head and look instead for absolutes. Make a list of villains who didn't possess any redeeming qualities and a list of heroes who were not flawed in any way. Then hand your lists to a friend and see if they can find the villains' redeeming qualities and heroes' flaws.

Applications: This exercise teaches you to see characters in their entirety. When you can see the good, the bad, and the ugly in real people (and other writers' characters), your own characters and subjects will be more believable.

3.9 Animal House

Not all characters in a piece of writing are people. Writers often have to decide how to handle animals and other nonhuman entities. In fiction, nonhuman characters often seem human. Animals, robots, vehicles, and even houses all become important characters if you anthropomorphize them.

The Exercise

For this exercise, you'll do a character sketch for a nonhuman character (see exercise 3.4 for tips on writing a character sketch), but you'll take it a step further and also write a scene. Your job is to make a nonhuman feel human to the reader.

Tips: The scene is more important than the character sketch, so if you have to cut corners, skip the sketch. Invest your time and energy into writing a scene that brings this character to life.

Variations: If you don't have time to make up a character, write a scene starring your pet. If you don't have a pet, write a scene starring one of your favorite nonhuman characters from the world of fiction.

Applications: Bestowing human qualities on animals and inanimate objects is an especially useful skill for anyone who wants to write for children or in genres such as science fiction and fantasy. However, this technique comes in handy in other ways, too. A human character might perceive or treat an inanimate object as if it's a person. We've all seen characters who name their cars or computers. We may even know people in real life who do such things. These are great quirks that make characters more realistic.

3.10 Your Gang

Writing about one or two people in a story or piece of nonfiction isn't too hard. Even a scene with three or four characters can be well executed by a beginning writer. When you start approaching casts and ensembles with seven, eight, nine primary characters, you risk turning your story into a riot. Everybody gets out of control.

Ensemble stories in fiction tend to be epics; they span long periods of time (sometimes several generations). Often in these stories, there are many main characters but only a few are in focus at any given time. You're more likely to find a good ensemble on television or in a movie than in a novel. But in all mediums, there are great stories about groups and families.

Writing a true ensemble piece requires considerable mastery in writing. As the author, you have to constantly keep all your characters in play, rotating them and managing their complex personalities. You can't forget about any of your characters, and you can't let any of them hog the spotlight. It's a balancing act.

The Exercise

Choose an existing ensemble from a book, movie, or TV show and write a long scene or a short story featuring all of the characters. Don't retell some story about the characters from the source material. Take the existing characters and make up your own story or scene for them.

As an added challenge, relocate the characters to a different setting. For example, take the cast from a book and put them in the setting of a movie.

The minimum number of characters you should work with for this exercise is six. Aim for eight.

Tips: You can write big scenes with all characters present (a dinner party would be a good setting for this). You can also put the characters in different locations and write a series of scenes that take place in these various locations. One example would be a huge family gathering for a holiday weekend. The characters will disperse to different rooms. You have to move through the house showing the reader what everyone is doing, and it all has to tie together in a meaningful way.

Variations: Come up with your own ensemble. Write a series of short character sketches and establish a setting in which these characters would be thrown together. They could be family, coworkers, passengers on a subway, or students in a classroom. You can also attempt this exercise with real people and write a scene from a real-life experience or make up a scene featuring your friends and family (a holiday gathering, school field trip, or work meeting). Make sure you give all the characters equal weight. Remember, it's an ensemble.

Applications: If you can write an ensemble scene, you might be suited for television writing!

Chapter 4: Speak Up

Dialogue and scripts

4.1 Basic Dialogue

Relationships are established, in large part, through conversation. Our verbal exchanges with others lead to friendship, romance, and conflict. Good dialogue does the same thing. It moves the action of a story forward. It reveals truths about the characters in the story. Most importantly, good dialogue feels real, even if it's not.

If you transcribe a natural conversation between two or more people, place quotation marks around their comments, and add a few dialogue tags, your narrative will fall flat on its face. That's because good written dialogue feels like real speech, but it's all an illusion. If you read dialogue closely, you'll realize that people just don't talk that way. We talk in bits and fragments. But our true, natural speech doesn't translate well to writing, so we improvise. We writers work our magic to make dialogue feel genuine.

Even in nonfiction books, such as memoirs, the dialogue is rarely (if ever) presented word for word as it was originally spoken. While many memoirists keep journals, and a few may have even recorded key conversations, they have to do their best to recall what was said, and many of them are open about the fact that the dialogue represents their best recollections.

It's worth noting that most dialogue, and certainly the best dialogue, is interwoven with action. As they speak, characters do things. They open the fridge and grab a beer. They fiddle with their shoelaces. They make faces and gestures. Not all communication happens verbally, and we rarely sit still when we talk to other people.

The Exercise

Write a scene that centers on a conversation between two people or characters. You can write fiction or nonfiction. If you're writing nonfiction, then recall an important or memorable conversation you had or overheard and re-create it. If you're writing fiction, then get a couple of your characters together for a discussion.

Tips: Make sure you punctuate your dialogue correctly. Don't get too creative with dialogue tags. In other words, stay away from tags like *he retorted, she muttered, he whispered, she stated.* Nothing beats the tried-and-true *he said* and *she said.*

Variations: As an alternative, test the claim that real conversation does not translate to good dialogue. Record a conversation (or find one that has already been recorded) and then transcribe a page or two. Make sure you use an actual conversation, not an interview. Read the piece aloud and observe why it does not work as narrative. When you're done, try reworking it into a good piece of dialogue.

Applications: Dialogue is present in most forms of writing. It even occurs in journalism, although in that form, dialogue is technically called "quotes" and must adhere strictly to what a person actually said. In stories (true or fictional), dialogue adds realism and encourages the reader to engage more closely with the narrative, because they feel like they are in on the conversation.

4.2 The Silver Screen

In some ways, a screenplay is easier to write than a novel. Screenplays tend to be shorter and more concise. They are usually around 120 pages (one page for each minute of film). A screenplay is highly condensed and doesn't require a lot of description. The writer doesn't have to worry about prose and voice because a screenplay is comprised of setting, action, and dialogue.

On the other hand, a screenplay has to be tight and as close to perfect as possible, and screenplay formatting is notoriously strict. If you don't follow proper formatting, nobody in the film industry will look at it.

If you see stories in your head as a series of moving pictures (rather than hearing stories as words), then screenwriting might be for you. If you struggle with complex grammar and long sentences or descriptions, or if you prefer to tell a story simply and straightforwardly, then screenwriting just might be your thing.

The Exercise

Keeping in mind that in a screenplay, one page equals one minute, write a five-minute script. It can be part of a greater story, or it can be a short film. It can even be an advertisement.

Tips: Before you start, take a quick look at screenplay formatting. A quick search online will bring up formatting rules and examples of screenplays that are properly formatted. Learning proper screenplay formatting is beyond the scope of this exercise, but you should certainly be aware of it.

Variations: If you're struggling for ideas, then try writing a script based on a scene from your favorite book or short story. This is called an adaptation.

Applications: There are many opportunities in the world of writing scripts. Movies and television shows are the most glamorous options, but some scriptwriters make commercials, promotional videos, or tutorials. With videos and film getting cheaper and easier to make every day, good scriptwriters are going to be in increasingly high demand.

4.3 Body Language

Sometimes what people say without actually speaking tells us a whole lot more than what comes out of their mouths. Using body language to communicate is natural. We all understand it intuitively—some better than others.

As a writer, you can closely observe people's body language and learn how humans speak without words, so you can bring unspoken communication into your writing.

Imagine two characters, a man and woman who are complete strangers, both shopping in a bookstore. You wouldn't write *Their eyes locked. They were instantly attracted to each other.* That would be boring and unimaginative. Instead, you would let the scene unfold and describe it to the reader—how their eyes met, how he gulped and she blushed, how they both suddenly felt warm, how the two of them slowly worked their way toward the center of the store until they finally met in the horror section.

The Exercise

Write a scene between two (or more) characters in which there is no dialogue, but the characters are communicating with each other through body language. You can also write a nonfiction piece. Surely you have experienced nonverbal communication. Take that experience and describe it on the page.

The scene should comprise at least two pages of interaction without dialogue, showing two or more characters engaging with each other. Here are a few scene starters:

- A cop, detective, or private investigator is tailing a suspect through a small town, big city, mall, amusement park, or other public area.

- Strangers are always good sources for ideas about communicating with body language. Think about where strangers are brought together: public transportation, classes, elevators, and formal meetings.

- Kids in a classroom aren't supposed to be speaking while a teacher is giving a lecture, but they always find ways to communicate.

Tips: What if one character misinterprets another character's body language? That could lead to humor or disaster. Maybe the characters are supposed to be doing something (like in a classroom where they're supposed to be listening to the teacher), but instead they're making faces and gestures at each other. Don't tell the reader what *he thought* or *she wondered* as these constructs are thought dialogue.

Variations: As an alternative, write a scene in which one character speaks and one doesn't: an adult and a baby, a human and an animal.

Applications: There are depictions of nonverbal communication in almost all types of storytelling from journalism and biography to memoir and fiction.

4.4 Love Scenes

Love is the most sought after of all human emotions. We have tons of clichés to express our love of love: it makes the world go round, it lasts forever, and it keeps us together. In songs, movies, poems, films, and novels—the most popular central theme is love.

Love scenes can be cheesy, mechanical, tender, or passionate. One thing is certain: nothing captivates a reader like a well-written love scene. It doesn't matter if the people in the scene are having a one-night stand or are long-lost lovers. If it's well written, your readers will respond to it.

Sex: it's what people do. Single people, married people, young people, and old people. Sex is an inherent component in many love scenes, and often, it's central to a love scene.

However, love scenes are not always about sex. In fact, love scenes aren't always between lovers. Love can be romantic, familial, fraternal, or patriotic. A love scene can be a first kiss or a last kiss. It can be a tender moment between friends or relatives. In fact, sweet, emotional exchanges are some of the best love scenes.

The Exercise

Write a love scene that demonstrates two people expressing their love and adoration for each other. Make sure the scene includes dialogue and action. Use an experience from your own life as inspiration or make one up.

Tips: The magic word is *love*, not *sex*. There's a genre for fiction that is sexual in nature: erotica. The idea here is to show two people expressing their love for each other through intimate words and actions.

Variations: Some people have a lot of love for inanimate objects. People love their cars, gadgets, clothes, and other possessions. It's not uncommon for people to express love for objects with sentimental value. As an alternative, write a scene depicting a character who loves an inanimate object.

Applications: Love happens all the time, every day. It's all around us. Unless you're writing scientific textbooks, there's a good chance love will enter the equation of your writing at some point. You need to know how to depict it.

In stories that aren't romance or love stories, readers enjoy a taste of affection between characters. Think of the best action, science fiction, fantasy, mystery, and horror stories. Love may not be the focus of the plot but it's there somewhere.

4.5 Multiple Speakers

It's hard to manage a crowd. When you have an ensemble of characters, and everybody's in the room at once, the narrative can be a nightmare to keep organized. If such scenes are not well executed, they can be impossible for readers to follow.

Sometimes it's necessary to write a scene that has a bunch of people all talking at once. This happens at meetings, family gatherings, in classrooms, and on public transportation.

It's critical in scenes like these to keep your narrative clear and organized. You cannot let the reader get confused about who's sitting where or which character is speaking.

The Exercise

First, you'll need to choose a situation in which there are several characters in one place. You should have at least six characters in play. Write out the scene, making sure each character gets at least two lines of dialogue and a few actions or gestures. Also, try to give the scene some purpose. In other words, don't simply transcribe what happened at your last office meeting if it was just another boring and meaningless meeting. But if it was the meeting where they laid off an entire department, then it will probably inspire some good storytelling.

Tips: The scene should be entertaining or meaningful, and in a novel, every scene should be relevant to the plot. One of the easiest ways to develop an entertaining scene is to turn an otherwise insignificant event into a major drama: a family is eating in a restaurant when one of them suddenly has a heart attack between the appetizers and the entrées.

Variations: If writing the scene in prose gets confusing, use a simple script format.

Applications: If you can manage dialogue between a group of characters in a single scene, you've got serious writing chops. Group scenes are among the most challenging to execute clearly and effectively.

4.6 He Said, She Said

Have you ever been reading a story and got so lost in the dialogue that you didn't know which character was speaking? Have you ever lost track of which character the pronoun referred to? For example, you're reading a story about three women who are best friends. Sometimes when the narrative refers to *her* or *she*, you're not sure who it's supposed to be.

In scenes with lengthy conversations between characters, the dialogue tags (*he said* or *she said*) can feel monotonous to the writer. It's tempting to start using creative tags: *she uttered, he mentioned,* or *she retorted.* These rarely enhance the narrative; usually, they are a distraction.

Readers are trained to the whole *he said* and *she said* dialogue format. They know these are cues that tell them who's saying what. They don't really register in the reader's mind as part of the story. So while they feel repetitive as you're writing, they're actually not.

However, there are instances in which it's better to use *she asked* or *he replied*. If a character screams or shouts, then you might want to specify that in the dialogue tags; you can also use exclamation marks.

Note that in dialogue tags, *he* and *she* will often be replaced with character names: *Tom said, Jane said.*

The Exercise

Write a dialogue scene with at least three characters having a conversation. It could be three coworkers, three kids playing in the woods, or three members of a family. Make sure the scene takes place in a setting where the characters can simply talk. In other words, they shouldn't be running through the jungle or anything like that. The objective is to make the dialogue smooth. It should always be clear who is speaking.

Tips: Since you have three characters, two will be of the same gender, so you have to watch your pronouns. Use character names in dialogue tags, but not exclusively; alternate between character names and pronouns. Also, note that the subject comes before the verb and the person opens their mouth before they speak: it's *Jane said, Tom said*, not *said Jane, said Tom*. Also, you're writing a scene, so intersperse the dialogue with action. Show the characters doing things while they're talking. One might get up and pace the room. Another might sweep her hair out of her eyes.

Variations: If three characters are too many and you're getting hung up on pronouns, then scale it back to two characters of the same gender. Try three later. If three characters are easy, add more.

Applications: Clarity is essential. The reader must always know which character is acting or speaking. This applies anytime you write dialogue, whether in a biography, a memoir, or a novel.

4.7 Quoteworthy

One of the greatest achievements a writer can make is writing prose that is quoteworthy. Many great lines and slang words or phrases have come to us from plays, books, poems, and movies.

In *Star Wars*, every so often, one of the characters says, "I've got a bad feeling about this." Every time someone says that, they're about to face a conflict. Those characters are awfully intuitive! This line caught on with the public. *Star Wars* fans grew up and became writers, and in tribute to their favorite movie, they might have one of *their* characters say, "I've got a bad feeling about this" right before something bad is about to happen.

Every generation has its memorable quotes. In the nineties, *Forrest Gump* told us, "Life is like a box of chocolates: you never know what you're going to get." In the eighties, *Top Gun* gave us "the need for speed." Even today, most people are familiar with a quote from the 1939 film *Gone with the Wind:* "Frankly my dear, I don't give a damn."

Quotes from novels are less likely to become famous than quotes from movies, probably because we'll watch a good movie over and over (heck, it's only two hours), many more times than we are inclined to read a book—even a book we love. Yet hundreds of years after his death, Shakespeare's most memorable lines are widely known:

- Romeo, Romeo, wherefore art thou Romeo?

- What's in a name? That which we call a rose / By any other name would smell as sweet;

- Parting is such sweet sorrow…

These are all from just one play by William Shakespeare (*Romeo and Juliet)*.

The Exercise

Come up with a list of three to five catchy and memorable lines or bits of dialogue. Wait—that's not all. You also have to provide context. It's not enough that Rhett Butler says "Frankly my dear, I don't give a damn." What matters, what makes the quote so memorable, is that he says it as he walks away from the woman he loves, and in that line, Rhett has finally given up on her (and given her up). It's a *moment.* Your quoteworthy lines have to be placed in pivotal moments.

Tips: Context is everything. If you establish a situation before you develop your quoteworthy lines, this exercise will be much easier. Start the exercise by placing your characters in a situation.

Variations: If you find yourself sitting there for over an hour, and you haven't come up with anything you think is quoteworthy, do not give up! Instead, set a goal to *find* three to five quoteworthy lines in the next few novels you read.

If that proves to be too much, then look for quoteworthiness in movies and TV shows. However, don't include quotes that are already famous.

Applications: The purpose of this exercise is not to push you to write dialogue that everyone runs around quoting and repeating. The purpose is to think about dialogue as an opportunity to 1) give your characters strong and memorable voices, and 2) make the narrative punchier and more captivating.

4.8 Character Chat

If you write fiction, your characters might occasionally behave like bratty, stubborn children who refuse to cooperate. Oh sure, you created the characters, so you think you have full control over them. But you will quickly learn that characters have minds of their own.

Your intention was for Charlie and Emily to fall in love, but Emily keeps looking at Josh with goo-goo eyes. *Cut it out, Emily! That's not the guy for you!* But she insists. Or you have a character who's supposed to save the world, except he's kind of a jerk and definitely a loser, and there's no way readers will believe this guy's going to risk himself to save anyone.

It's a bizarre phenomenon. But we are not puppeteers pulling our characters' strings. Well, actually, we can be. There's a word for writing like that: forced. When you try to cram a square character into a round mold, it feels unnatural. Readers pick up on that stuff, and it doesn't do you or your story any good.

So what do you do when your characters are committing anarchy?

Well, you could try talking to them.

The Exercise

You're going to have a little chat with one of your characters. Just open a document or pull out a sheet of paper. Say hello to your character, and then write the character's response. Keep going back and forth. Model the conversation after an Internet chat.

Tips: This is a good way to get to know your character before you start writing a story. If you can relax and get into a creative, Zenlike state, your character will, in fact, talk to you.

Variations: You might not want to speak directly to your character. Okay, fine. Instead, do a script-style dialogue between your character and some other character. This exercise happens outside of your manuscript or draft. In other words, it's not intended for publication or inclusion in your story. It's a getting-to-know-you exercise, and it will work if you simply write a scene between two characters or talk directly to them yourself.

Applications: You can use this exercise anytime your story or your characters are stuck.

4.9 Distinct Voices

Writers talk a lot about voice as an element of writing, and what they mean is the writer's voice or the style of the prose. In college-level literature courses, you might be asked to identify an author from a short excerpt. You're not expected to have memorized the author's entire repertoire. You are supposed to have read the author's work closely enough that you can recognize his or her voice.

Some writers and teachers say that voice cannot be taught. It comes with experience. The more you write, the more your voice will emerge.

Voices emerge from characters, too, except they emerge quickly, and if they don't, you have to find their voices or maybe give them their voices. One character might speak with a lot of slang while another uses quaint words and phrases. How your characters speak will depend on where they grew up, how educated they are, and what class or culture they belong to.

Geography, education, and culture aside, we all have our own way of speaking—that little special something that is uniquely ours. If you can give your characters unique voices, then you will be a master of dialogue.

The Exercise

Write a dialogue scene with two or more characters. Your objective is to give each character a distinct voice. In other words, if you remove all the surrounding narrative and dialogue tags, a reader will be able to identify who is speaking.

Tips: To test your exercise, remove everything from the scene except the dialogue. Take out the action, the descriptions, and the dialogue tags. Now, read it aloud. Can you tell which character is saying what? Give it to a friend to read. Can your friend identify two voices?

Variations: As an alternative, take a dialogue-heavy scene out of a novel or script and test it for yourself. Are the characters' voices distinct? If not, tweak them until they are.

Applications: Writing distinct dialogue adds to the overall voice of a narrative but more importantly, it makes characters more realistic.

4.10 Internal and External Dialogue

Some narratives tell us what characters are thinking. In a first-person narrative, the entire story is told by one of the characters, from his or her perspective (the viewpoint character is referred to as *I*). In a third-person narrative, the story is told by a narrator who is not a character in the story (all characters are referred to as *he, she,* or *they*).

Third-person point of view gives the author the most flexibility because the camera can see all the characters equally and objectively. In some cases, the narrative might get closer to certain characters and bring the reader inside those characters' thoughts. In these instances, it's like the camera is sitting on those characters' shoulders.

Narratives often share characters' thoughts with the reader. This is called thought dialogue:

- *I know,* she thought, *I'll write a book.*

- He thought she was talented.

Thought dialogue can be formatted in different ways. Traditionally, all spoken dialogue is placed in quotation marks, and thoughts are italicized. Some authors forgo punctuating and formatting dialogue and thoughts altogether, but the narrative has to be extremely clear and concise to pull this off without confusing readers with regard to who is thinking or speaking.

The Exercise

Write a scene in which three characters are having a conversation. The scene will be written in third person, but it will go inside one of the characters' heads and include that character's thought dialogue. That character will participate in the conversation through spoken dialogue, but the narrative will also give readers that character's inner thoughts via thought dialogue.

Tips: Use conventional punctuation and formatting: quotation marks for dialogue and italics for thoughts.

Make sure the thought dialogue is relevant to the scene or essential to the story.

Variations: Write the same scene in first person or use third person but include thought dialogue for all three characters. This is difficult to pull off, because you'll have three characters who are all talking and thinking at the same time.

Applications: Some writers avoid thought dialogue because it gives certain characters an advantage, and in third-person point of view, thought dialogue can feel like a cheat. Instead of showing the reader what is happening, thought dialogue often tells the reader by revealing what characters are thinking. However, it can be used effectively. When you've completed this exercise, review the scene you've written and decide whether the thought dialogue enriches or weakens the scene. Revise accordingly.

Chapter 5: Fiction

Making it up

5.1 World Building

In order for readers to visualize a piece of writing and put it in context of the world they know and understand, you, the writer, have to fully realize the story's setting. Does it take place in a metropolis or the countryside? Are the characters inside some virtual reality or on a distant planet? Does this tale take place a long time ago or in the far-off future?

The setting could be a real city (maybe the city in which you live) or it could be a made-up town or village. It can occur in the past, present, or future.

In historical fiction, we don't build worlds, but a historical setting requires research for accuracy. Writers must have a thorough understanding of the geography, culture, and significant events surrounding the time and place in which a story is set.

World building is when we invent our own setting.

Consider classic fantasies like *Alice in Wonderland* or *Peter Pan*, and the necessity for world building becomes clear. In speculative fiction, which includes science fiction and fantasy, world building often requires elaborate planning.

The Exercise

Create a world from scratch and write a one-page description for a speculative fiction story setting. First, you'll need to decide whether your story takes place in the past, present, or future. Next, determine how your world is different from the real world in which you're currently living. Is it populated with mythological creatures, like trolls, unicorns, and fairies? Are there aliens? Is your world a metropolis or a desolate, distant planet?

Tips: Here are some elements to include: geography and landscape, climate, culture, economics, trade, social (class) structure, and government systems.

Variations: Write a one-page overview of an existing fantastical world. You could describe Wonderland, Neverland, the Matrix, or the faraway galaxy from your favorite science fiction story. As another alternative, you can work on a historical setting. Historical fiction requires solid research, so make sure you get your facts right.

Applications: Setting is one of the key elements in fiction. It can also be important in nonfiction writing, especially when writing a memoir or any nonfiction project that deals with geography, ecology, or the environment.

5.2 Yourtopia

This exercise builds on the previous world-building exercise by asking you to go to extremes in creating a setting for your story.

Dystopia is a type of world that is dark and miserable. Humanity is suffering en masse. Dystopian fiction is often marked by disease, oppression, war, overcrowding, and human enslavement. Utopia is the opposite of dystopia. It's a world in which life is ideal. These worlds are somewhat subjective. One person's dystopia might be another person's utopia.

Exploring and inventing such worlds requires using your imagination and thinking in extremes. You're basically creating a world in which the worst possible scenario—or best possible scenario—has arisen. In these stories, the scales are tipped to good or evil.

The Exercise

Write a two-page overview of a dystopian or utopian world. For this exercise, you will create a future on earth, so your overview should include a brief history explaining how the world reached this dystopian or utopian state, as well as descriptions of the social systems and cultural structures.

Tips: Remember that the key to a dystopian—or a utopian—world is its extreme nature. One way to develop a dystopian setting would be to consider the harshest situations that humanity has endured throughout history and then bring them all together into a single world. Look for periods of enlightenment and prosperity, and combine those for a utopian setting.

Variations: If creating an entire world seems overwhelming or intimidating, try creating a smaller setting—a town or an island. As an alternative, make a list of fantastical worlds you've seen in fiction, TV, and movies. Then list elements of the world that are positive and negative.

Applications: Inventing such worlds is good practice in creating environments and for developing ideas for conflict and resolution. If the world itself naturally provides struggles for the characters, you've just found a good source of conflict.

5.3 Setting as Character

Does a place have personality? Is a city alive? Can it speak to us? Does it feel or think? How does a story's setting affect the characters?

Anthropomorphism is the practice of humanizing an inanimate object. Dancing teacups and talking appliances are examples of anthropomorphism in fiction. Humanizing a place is usually subtle. It doesn't dance, sing, or talk. When settings are humanized, they don't act as backdrops for a story; they act as characters. Such settings have personality and attitude.

In Anne McCaffrey's popular science fiction series, *The Dragonriders of Pern,* a group of humans find themselves establishing a colony on an unfamiliar planet. While the planet doesn't talk or take action (and the characters don't believe it can do these things), it is given a clear personality.

Writers often characterize their settings, attributing traits to them that are normally reserved for people or characters. A city is mean, a house is friendly, a street is lonely.

The Exercise

Choose a setting for a story. It can be a room, a building, a town, or an entire planet. It can be a real place or a place you've made up. Next, write a character sketch for this place.

Tips: Review exercise 3.4 for tips on creating a character sketch. Use those tips to give your fictional setting human traits.

Variations: If you'd rather write a bit of narrative instead of a sketch, then write a short scene in which the setting of your story is the central character.

Applications: Setting as character is actually pretty rare, but when it's executed well, it captures readers' imaginations. If you've ever read a story about someplace and wished you could go there, then you know how a powerful setting can engage and inspire readers.

5.4 Fictionalize It

Real life gets fictionalized all the time. When people tell stories, they often embellish to make the events in their stories more exciting. A feral cat becomes a bobcat. A five-foot drop becomes a twenty-story fall. And a bad day becomes the worst day ever.

Sometimes we fictionalize real life by accident. In the game of telephone, all the players sit or stand in a line. The first person writes down a statement and then whispers it into the next person's ear. Each person whispers the statement to the next person in line, and when it gets to the last person, he or she says aloud whatever was whispered into their ear. It never matches what was originally written down.

Rumors and legends are often the result of accidental games of telephone. Something happens, and people start talking about it. As they spread the word, they misinterpret or misunderstand what they originally heard, and eventually, the story loses its accuracy.

Sometimes we fictionalize reality on purpose. If you've ever read a book or seen a movie that was "based on a true story," you saw real life fictionalized. These stories use real events but embellish them to make the tale more interesting.

The Exercise

Think about a significant event that you experienced. It could be the day your parents came home with a baby brother or sister or the time you won the school spelling bee. Write a short outline of what happened, and then make some sweeping embellishments. The goal here is to make drastic changes: alter the setting, characters, plot, or sequence of events. Instead of a baby brother or sister, maybe your parents came home with triplets. Instead of taking place in the school's gymnasium, the spelling bee was held someplace exciting, like a theme park or a national monument. Update your outline with the embellishments you've made.

Tips: As you write your outline, focus on listing the actual actions and events that occurred. You wake up, take a shower, have breakfast, and then go to the spelling bee. But there's more to it than that. When you wake up, you also turn off your alarm clock. Instead of simply taking a shower, you undress, wash, dry off, and then dress. You must prepare breakfast before you eat it. And what do you do with your breakfast dishes? Focus on the little steps that comprise each action in the sequence. Often that is where embellishments work best. An alarm that doesn't go off or a broken dish can make a story more realistic and more interesting. These details can also lead to story developments. For example, an alarm clock that doesn't go off might cause you to be late.

Variations: As an alternative to using a day in your life, look to the news or a documentary for a real event that you can fictionalize by embellishing details.

Applications: Many fiction writers base stories or characters on real life and then get overly attached to reality. Why write fiction at all? These stories often end up feeling forced or contrived. The beauty of fiction is in finding the truth rather than telling it. Real life is a wondrous source of inspiration; embellishments make fiction writing delicious.

5.5 It's All in the Details

When you're writing, one simple detail can tell a reader more than a full page of dull, drawn-out description. This is especially true in fiction, where you're working with made-up material and need to get the reader to believe in it.

Detail is important on every level. Whether you're introducing a character, describing a setting, or going through an action sequence, the little things will give your story much needed realism.

For example, you can write a lengthy description of a character's appearance and include descriptions of hair color, skin tone, facial shape, eye color, physical build, and each article of clothing the character wears. By the time the description is complete, the reader is fast asleep. It's more effective to use a few, key details that are unique to that character and are the most memorable things about his appearance:

Greasy strands of black hair hung around his scrawny, pockmarked face. His teeth were yellow and crooked, and he wore a stained tee shirt with a picture of a beer bottle on it.

The Exercise

Choose a character and a setting and write a scene in which both are revealed through descriptive detail.

The scene should not be a long description of your character or setting; rather, it should be a scene with action, dialogue, and purpose, but in which vivid, meaningful details about your character and setting are revealed.

Tips: Use clear, interesting, and sharp descriptions. Keep these descriptions to a minimum, but use rich details so that they are clear in the reader's mind. When you've completed your draft, revise and edit it to make the details in the piece as clear and memorable as possible.

Variations: Instead of writing a scene, develop a character or establish a setting with an emphasis on detail.

Applications: Knowing which details to include in a piece of writing can be tricky. Writers and readers have different preferences for how much detail they want. Working closely with the details and descriptions in a story helps you become more aware of what works (or adds to the story) and what doesn't.

5.6 Fan Fiction

All around the world, there are fan communities comprised of people who are totally obsessed. Some are obsessed with rock stars and sports celebrities. Others are obsessed with products. (Surely you've met an Apple user?) As you have probably guessed, we're concerned with fans who are obsessed with stories.

When fans write fiction set in a famous or popular story world, it is known as fan fiction. Most fan fiction is found in science fiction and fantasy, but it is found in other genres, too. Fan fiction is more popular for works that appeared in film and television, but novels have also spawned fan fiction.

For the most part, fan-fiction writing is a hobby. It's almost never published commercially. And before you write fan fiction, you should know a few things about copyright law.

You can, of course, write whatever you want privately. You can rewrite the ending to a movie that disappointed you or make the lead character in your favorite romance fall in love with someone else. What happens in your notebook is not subject to copyright law, but as soon as you share, distribute, or publish your fan fiction, the law becomes relevant.

When an author writes a novel, the world and characters of the story become that author's intellectual property. Story elements in a movie or TV show are also owned by some entity, usually the network or studio that produced it. Basically, the story, plot, and characters all belong to somebody.

Some intellectual property owners are strictly opposed to fan fiction. If they find fan fiction being published in any way, shape, or form, they might take legal action. Others are lenient. In many cases, as long as fan fiction writers are not making money off the work, they'll let it slide. A few might pick and choose. If you take their heroes and turn them into serial killers, you could get a letter from their lawyers.

Fortunately, most intellectual-property owners embrace fan fiction. They understand that fan fiction celebrates and pays tribute to their work, and they also realize that fan fiction is a form of free publicity.

The Exercise

Think about one of your favorite stories. It can be a movie, television show, or novel. Now, write a scene set somewhere in that story's world. For this exercise, do not change anything that happened in the original story.

Tips: In fan fiction, there are no rules. You could rewrite some part of a story, but most fan fiction explores the existing story further, instead of trying to change what already happened. In some fan-fiction communities, changing the canon is frowned upon. For this exercise, you can use existing characters and write a scene that takes place after the story ended, or you can create new characters and set them in the world of the story (this works well for science fiction and fantasy).

If fan fiction intrigues you, search for fan fiction communities online.

Variations: Instead of writing a single scene, write an outline for a longer story. What will the next installment of your favorite series look like?

Applications: Fan fiction is great for beginning fiction writers, because most of the story elements are provided for you: the world, the characters, and a history are already established. This allows you to practice writing dialogue and action without worrying about creating characters and worlds.

Be aware that fan fiction is not likely to get published, but there are a few exceptions. Sometimes, an author will team up with fans who are writers and publish collaborative stories. And you never know—if you make it big or get lucky, you could write the next story in your favorite franchise.

Fan-fiction communities help you improve your writing, network with other writers, and connect with fans of a work you admire—people like you.

5.7 Symbols and Symbolism

In *Alice and Wonderland*, a white rabbit appears, and Alice follows him down a rabbit hole that leads to Wonderland. In the story, the white rabbit is a herald—a character archetype that signifies the first challenge or the call to adventure. This is the change in the main character's life that marks the beginning of the story.

The white rabbit became so widely known that it eventually evolved into a symbol. Because it's white, it can symbolize purity. Because it's a rabbit, it can symbolize fertility. But because it was the herald that called Alice to her adventure, the white rabbit is often used as a symbol to represent change. Sometimes, it's simply used as a herald.

The white rabbit appeared in *The Matrix,* an episode of *Star Trek,* and in several episodes of *Lost.* In *Jurassic Park*, a character finds a file labeled "whiterabbit.obj" and in Stephen King's *The Long Walk*, a character refers to himself as "the white rabbit type."

The white rabbit can function as a traditional symbol or as a reference to *Alice in Wonderland.* Such is the case with the song "White Rabbit" by Jefferson Airplane.

Symbolism occurs whenever one thing represents something else. For example, a book could represent knowledge. A caged bird could represent oppression or imprisonment. In a story, the repetition of a symbol (every time the book or caged bird appears) can have significance to the story. Maybe every time a character fails because he doesn't know enough, there's a book in the scene. Or perhaps a person who is oppressed keeps a caged bird but doesn't recognize the irony (that he is imprisoning a living creature while suffering his own oppression).

The Exercise

Develop a list of five to ten symbols. Invent your own symbols rather than using ones that commonly appear in fiction. If you're working on a story or novel, make a list of symbols that you might use in your project. Symbols are often linked to big themes: love, revenge, sacrifice, redemption, narcissism, etc.

Tips: You might find it easier to choose a theme or issue and then look for a symbol that represents it. On the other hand, if you have an interesting image (a red scarf, a snow globe), you might find a way to turn it into a meaningful symbol.

Variations: Choose one symbol and write a list of ways that it can be used throughout a story. How many ways could you bring a white rabbit into a story? It could be seen in a pet store. It could be somebody's pet. It could be in a science lab. It could be part of a magic show. Make sure you don't give the symbol more importance than the plot or characters. A symbol is present to add depth and give the story greater meaning. It's an accent to the story, not the central focus of it.

Applications: Symbols enrich a piece of writing, adding layers to the themes and meaning of the piece.

5.8 Unbelievable!

Fiction writers often ask readers to believe the unbelievable. Even stories that are not fantastical contain elements that are so unlikely, most people won't believe it unless the piece is deftly written.

For example, in sitcoms, it's common to use a misunderstanding as a comedic device. Two characters who are married to other people are seen coming out of a hotel together. A third character happens to be driving by and immediately concludes they are having an affair. The third character then struggles with whether to confront them, tell their spouses, or mind her own business. Laughs ensue because the audience is in on the joke: the two characters were planning a surprise party for one of their spouses and had rented a ballroom inside the hotel.

In real life, such misunderstandings may happen occasionally, but usually they get worked out without a bunch of comedy and drama. If the third character is close enough to the others to be concerned, she would normally know about the surprise party and would therefore know why the two were at the hotel together, or the third character would realize that what she saw may not mean they are having an affair, so she would do a little checking before drawing conclusions about what's really going on.

In fantastical fiction, writers convince readers of extremely farfetched notions: zombies, wizards, aliens, fairies, vampires, time travel, and unicorns, to name a few.

Some fiction doesn't require readers to suspend disbelief. In fact, some stories are so easily believable that they could just as well be true. For this exercise, you'll stay away from stories like those.

The Exercise

Come up with an unlikely scenario, something that most people would roll their eyes at and say *yeah, right*. In the case of a misunderstanding, we often think the third character is silly, stupid, or not thinking clearly, because she made such a shortsighted assumption based on what she saw.

Come up with a scenario that's as unlikely as possible. It can be as simple as a misunderstanding, or it can be as elaborate as an alien race living in the New York sewer system.

Once you have your scenario, write a short scene. This is where you should focus on making readers believe the unbelievable.

Tips: One way to make the impossible seem believable is through detail. It's hard to believe there are aliens living in the New York sewer system, but if you can explain what they look like, how they live, and where they came from, then you just might be convincing.

Variations: If you can't come up with an unbelievable scenario or premise, borrow one from a famous story. Instead of writing a scene, examine the piece you've chosen and identify the details and techniques the writer used to make it believable.

Applications: It's hard enough to convince the public of the truth, thus the saying: truth is stranger than fiction. A writer who can convince readers to suspend disbelief for the duration of a story has acquired one of the most magical skills that any writer can possess: the ability to create illusions.

5.9 Potter Wars

A lot of artists struggle with the desire to write original material. Of course we all want to be original, but is that even possible?

Some say there are no new stories, just remixed and rehashed versions of stories we're all familiar with. When we say a piece of writing is original, a close examination will reveal that it has roots in creative works that preceded it.

Most of us writers have had ideas that we shunned because we thought they were too similar to other stories. But just because your story idea is similar to another story, perhaps a famous one, should you give up on it?

Look at this way: everything already exists. The ideas, plots, and characters—they're already out there in someone else's story. Originality isn't a matter of coming up with something new, it's a matter of using your imagination to take old concepts and put them together in new ways.

To test this theory, see if you can guess the following famous story:

> *A young orphan who is being raised by his aunt and uncle receives a mysterious message from a stranger. This leads him on a series of great adventures. Early on, he receives training to learn superhuman skills. Along the way, he befriends loyal helpers, specifically a guy and a gal who end up falling for each other. Our hero is also helped by a number of nonhuman creatures. His adventures lead him to a dark and evil villain who is terrorizing everyone and everything that our hero knows and loves.*

If you guessed that this synopsis outlines *Harry Potter*, then you guessed right. But if you guessed that it was *Star Wars*, you're also right.

This shows how two stories that are extremely different from each other can share many similarities, including basic plot structure and character relationships, and it proves that writing ideas will manifest in different ways when executed by different writers.

If it's true that originality is nothing more than putting together old concepts in new ways, then instead of giving up on a project that you think has been done before, you should simply try to make it your own by giving it a new twist.

The Exercise

Use the synopsis above to write your own short story. However, do not write a space opera or a tale about wizards.

Tips: One of the key differences between *Star Wars* and *Harry Potter* is the setting. One is set in a galaxy far, faraway; the other in a magical school for wizards. One is science fiction; the other is fantasy. Start by choosing a completely different genre and setting, and you'll be off to a good start. For example, you could write a Western or a romance.

Variations: Instead of writing a short story, write a detailed outline for a novel or novella.

Applications: This exercise is designed to demonstrate the following:

- It's not unusual for two writers to come up with similar ideas.

- A vague premise or concept will be executed differently by different writers.

- Instead of worrying about original characters and plots, focus on combining well-known elements in new ways.

5.10 The Elevator Pitch

If you want to pitch your fiction to a publisher or an agent, then you need to be convincing and concise. And if you want to pitch your fiction to readers, you have to make it sound captivating. You have to entice everyone.

In describing your fiction, you must first be aware of genres in publishing, and you should be able to place your work in appropriate categories.

Some writers loathe the genre model, and with good reason. Genres are confining. What if you want to write a story about aliens that explores the human condition and is written in verse? Is it literary fiction, science fiction, or poetry? Where would your story be shelved or categorized?

On the other hand, genres make it easier to market fiction, and they help readers find the types of stories they like best. If you love fantasy but dislike romance, you know which section of the bookstore to visit. Without these labels, finding good books to read would be a hassle.

The Exercise

Choose a story you've written or one of the exercises you've completed in this book, and write a short pitch for it with a focus on genre. Read aloud, your pitch should be about thirty seconds long (the length of an elevator ride). Make sure you identify the genre and include a brief description of your story's premise. Focus on making your pitch enticing. Don't include any major spoilers. In other words, it should make people want to read your story, without giving too much away.

Tips: Be as specific as possible. For the story you choose, list all of the genres that apply to your story. If necessary, conduct research about bookstore categories and genres in literature. Then, choose the single best genre or category for your story. If necessary, you can also identify a subcategory or two.

Variations: If you don't have a project to use for this exercise, then write a pitch for your favorite book.

Applications: If you write fiction and intend to get your work published, you'll have to pitch it at some point. There's no way around this, and the better you can sell your stories, the more of your stories you'll be able to sell.

Chapter 6: Storytelling

Once upon a time, someone, somewhere lived happily ever after

6.1 The Three-Act Structure

Every good story has a beginning, middle, and end. In the beginning, we meet the characters and learn about their problems. In the middle, those problems persist as the characters struggle through ongoing conflict. At the end, the main conflict is resolved. That's storytelling in a nutshell.

While there are other models that can be used in storytelling, the three-act structure is the simplest and most common. It is broken down as follows:

Act 1: Introduction or setup
Act 2: Rising action (conflict)
Act 3: Resolution

The three-act structure is used in writing novels, movies, plays, and all other forms of storytelling. It helps writers make sure they have the essential elements in their structure and provides a framework through which we can discuss, evaluate, and analyze a story.

The classic example of a three-act story is boy meets girl:

Act 1: Boy meets girl (setup)
Act 2: Boy loses girl and tries to get her back (rising action)

Act 3: Boy gets girl back (resolution)

This is the foundation of almost every romance and love story, and there is an infinite number of variations.

The Exercise

Using the boy-meets-girl model as a starting point, write five to ten ideas for stories based on the three-act structure. You do not have to write romance, but be sure to include a beginning, middle, and end (setup, rising action, and resolution).

Tips: Avoid going into too much detail. You don't need to create character sketches, outlines, and scenes. Keep it as simple as possible.

Variations: Choose five to ten books and films and break them down into their three-act structures. This forces you to whittle your favorite stories down to their bare bones.

Applications: The three-act structure is used in storytelling for all mediums and also in discussing and analyzing a story comprehensively. It is, perhaps, the most important foundation in storytelling that all writers should be familiar with.

6.2 The Hero's Journey

The hero's journey is complex enough to provide fodder for an entire book of fiction and character-writing exercises. It is essentially a formula for storytelling that was not developed but discovered.

Acclaimed mythologist Joseph Campbell discovered that across all cultures throughout history, there are specific plot points and character archetypes that occur in the greatest myths, legends, and other tales. These comprise the hero's journey, which is also sometimes called the monomyth.

The original structure has seventeen stages, and many variations have been culled from Campbell's discovery. For this exercise, we'll work with one of the most widely used variations, a twelve-stage structure developed by Christopher Vogler. This variation started as a memo that made its way around Hollywood.

Here's an adaptation of Vogler's twelve stages of the hero's journey:

1. **Home or starting place:** We are introduced to the hero in his or her home or starting place.

2. **Call to adventure:** The hero's world undergoes a dramatic shift, either by an external force (the villain) or by some change within the hero's heart or mind.

3. **Refusal of the call:** The hero resists the call to adventure or refuses to accept a role in the forthcoming challenge.

4. **Meeting the mentor:** The hero meets someone with knowledge or experience and receives training or supplies that will be required for the adventure.

5. **Acceptance of the call:** The hero finally accepts the call and resolves to leave home to embark on the adventure, entering a new space or state of mind.

6. **Friends, foes, and tests:** The hero acquires allies or helpers. Foes are established, and allegiances are determined. The hero is tested.

7. **Approaching the underworld:** The hero and his or her helpers get ready for the first big challenge.

8. **Ordeal in the underworld**: The hero enters the underworld and faces death (this can be symbolic), but will emerge reborn or with a new understanding or purpose.

9. **Reward:** There is a reward for overcoming the ordeal and surviving the underworld.

10. **Preparing for the return:** The hero prepares to return home; the last leg of the mission lies ahead. The tension is reaching its peak.

11. **Climax:** There is a final obstacle or challenge at the climax. The stakes are higher than ever. The hero makes a sacrifice, suffers a loss, or undergoes another death and rebirth.

12. **Resolution and return:** The conflict is finally resolved. The hero returns home (this can be a symbolic homecoming), having grown and bearing knowledge or items (treasure) that will change the world for the better.

You can read the full twelve stages from Christopher Vogler's memo by visiting www.thewritersjourney.com.

The Exercise

Give the hero's journey a spin. You don't have to write a full manuscript; just outline twelve movements for a story adhering to the formula above. It can be a novel, short story, play, or movie.

Tips: If you want to master the hero's journey, pick up a book or research it online. Wikipedia lists the full seventeen stages from Campbell's original work.

Variations: As an alternative to creating your own outline based on the hero's journey, read a book or watch a movie, and list the stages of the hero's journey for that story. Some suggested stories and films for this exercise: *Star Wars, Harry Potter, The Wizard of Oz, The Matrix, Titanic, Robin Hood.*

Applications: While some writers think formulaic writing is too commercial or contrived, formulas and structures are useful for writers. Writing a novel or a full-length movie is an incredibly involved process, and any help is good help. Formulas can ensure that your story is not missing something essential. It also helps you create a story with familiar patterns that resonate with audiences.

In terms of formulas, the hero's journey is unique, in that it was discovered in cultures across time and space, which means it is a foundation for writing a story that is timeless and universal.

6.3 Narrative and Point of View

The simplest definition of narrative is only one word: story. Narrative is the text of the story (words and sentences), as well as the setting, characters, dialogue, and plot. It's the sequence of events. Narrative is the whole shebang.

A good narrative is structured. It has a beginning, a middle, and an end. It also has a point of view, which is the perspective from which the story is told. The two most common points of view in narrative are first person and third person.

A first-person narrative is told from the perspective of a person or character inside the story. It's easily identifiable because there is an "I" or speaker relaying the story. First-person narrative is popular because it takes readers into the mind of the character whom the story is about. One of the most famous novels written in first person is *The Catcher in the Rye* by J. D. Salinger:

> If you really want to hear about it, the first thing you'll probably want to know is where I was born and what my lousy childhood was like, and how my parents were occupied and all before they had me, and all that David Copperfield kind of crap, but I don't feel like going into it, if you want to know the truth.

Third-person narrative offers a broader perspective and feels more like an outside observer is relaying the story. Many writers prefer third person because the perspective does not rely on any single character. Therefore, third-person point of view is more flexible.

Third-person narrative can be further classified into two axes:

1. The first axis is the subjective/objective mode. The subjective mode describes characters' thoughts and feelings, whereas objective mode does not.

2. The second axis is omniscient/limited. The omniscient point of view indicates a narrator that has full knowledge of all events, places, and time. A limited point of view is closely connected to a particular character in the story and cannot provide information or details about events or actions that the focal character is unaware of.

The Exercise

Choosing point of view for a story is a big decision. Some writers get several chapters into a book and then decide they need to change the point of view. That requires a lot of rewriting. You can do a quick exercise to experiment with point of view. Choose a story or piece of writing that you have completed. You'll work with the first page (or a one-page excerpt). If it's in third person, rewrite it in first person. If it's first person, rewrite it in third person.

Tips: You may find that changing the point of view requires revising the entire tone of the story. Changing point of view often changes the amount of information that the reader has access to. Does this help or hurt your story?

Variations: If you don't have a piece of writing that you can use for this exercise, then choose a short story or novel that you are familiar with and rewrite a scene. Try writing the scene in both axes and all four modes.

Applications: When we're writing a story, we can become so focused on plot and character that we forget to think carefully about how we style the narrative and which point of view is best for the story. This exercise requires that you deliberate on point of view and experiment with it to see how different points of view affect narrative.

6.4 Starting in the Middle (Nonlinear Storytelling)

Any decent narrative has a beginning, a middle, and an end. But here's a little storytelling secret: you can start your story in the middle of the action.

The premise of the television show *Lost* was that a plane crashed on an island. The show is the survivors' story. Many writers would be inclined to start the story either while the passengers are boarding the plane or while they're in the air, before the aircraft goes down.

The show's creators had a better idea. Start the story with a man waking up in the jungle *after the crash*. He's dazed. He gets up, stumbles around, and then runs out of the jungle to the beach, where the plane wreckage is burning and people are running around screaming.

The audience is thrust right into the middle of the action. *Lost* also used flashbacks to take the audience further back in time so they could experience the flight and the crash as well as the characters' distant pasts.

The lesson is that the beginning of your story may not be the same point where you actually choose to start telling it. Starting in the middle won't always work, and in truth, every beginning can be traced back to some other, previous beginning. The trick then is choosing the right moment in your story to introduce your setting, characters, and conflict.

The Exercise

Come up with a simple story (or use one you've already written). Write a short timeline detailing the chronological sequence of major events. This might be a list of scenes that comprise the story. Then write an outline, synopsis, or overview showing how you can start your story by jumping into the middle of the action. Now that the beginning has been lopped off, provide an explanation for how you will reveal it to readers.

Tips: Use note cards to organize and reorder your scenes.

Keep in mind that nonlinear storytelling doesn't always work. Avoid using it just for the sake of being creative.

Here are a few ideas to get you started:

- **Murder mystery.** Start the story when the detectives are already conducting the investigation rather than the standard, which is to start it when they get a call to the scene of the crime.

- **Love story.** Romances have become increasingly formulaic. The characters meet, fight their feelings, and then finally fall in love. Rearrange the order of events. Can you tell a love story that starts at the wedding and is told backward?

- **Hero's journey.** Exercise 6.2 outlines one variation of the hero's journey. Can you tweak the sequence and tell the story out of chronological order?

Variations: Use a story from a book, TV show (episode), or movie that you know well. Start by writing a list of key scenes. Then, rearrange the scenes and add transitions or additional scenes that help tell the story nonlinearly. You don't have to write out the narrative; an outline or synopsis will show you how nonlinear storytelling might work.

Applications: Nonlinear storytelling adds complexity and depth to a story. It's not for everyone and isn't appropriate for every story, but experimenting with it will show you how difficult it is to execute. You will also see what a useful device it can be and how severely it fails when used inappropriately.

6.5 Discovery Writing

Some writers swear by their outlines. If they know every twist and turn their story will take, they can focus on the details in the prose, dialogue, setting, and characters.

Other writers use discovery writing (which is often called pantsing, as in *writing by the seat of your pants*) because if they know where the story is going, they become too bored to bother writing it.

Discovery writing is the process of letting the story unfold as you're writing it. You start with a few characters and a setting, and you just start writing.

The characters take over, and you just follow along. Magically, a plot emerges.

Discovery writing may not work for all writers and may not be the best technique for all genres. For example, it might be difficult to write a good murder mystery if you don't start out knowing who did it. How will you plant clues and red herrings?

Even if you're the kind of person who works better with a plan, you should give discovery writing a try.

The Exercise

Choose a few characters (you can create new ones or use characters you've already created) and pick a setting. Do not plan any plot or action for your story—just start writing. Try to make your story at least three pages, but feel free to follow it for as long as necessary to get to the end.

Tips: There's no law that says you have to exclusively use outlining or discovery writing. In fact, you can use outlining to plan major milestones in your story and then use discovery writing to find your way to those milestones. There's no universal technique that works for all writers. Your best bet is to experiment with both outlining and discovery writing and figure out what works best for you. Most writers find that some combination of discovery writing and outlining is ideal.

Variations: If discovery writing stumps you or causes you to write in circles, then try establishing the ending and write toward it. If you're still stuck, then use the three-act structure (see exercise 6.1) and discovery write your way through those three acts.

Applications: Experimenting with different techniques is the only way you'll find the method that works best for you.

6.6 Chekhov's Gun

Chekhov's gun is a literary device in which an element is mentioned in a story and its purpose or significance becomes clear later. For example, early in a story, the narrative mentions that the protagonist carries a knife. Later, she uses that knife to defend herself in a fight. If the knife hadn't been mentioned earlier, it might feel like an object of convenience. On the other hand, if the knife is mentioned, but she never uses it, the reader might feel cheated after anticipating a good knife fight.

The real purpose of Chekhov's gun is to remind writers that they have an obligation to fulfill all promises made to readers. If the narrative mentions that the protagonist carries a knife, the reader expects that she will, at some point, use it. If she doesn't, the writer has failed to fulfill a promise. In other words, don't pepper your story with unnecessary, insignificant, or meaningless elements. Make everything count!

The term "Chekhov's gun" comes from a letter from Anton Chekhov to Aleksandr Semenovich Lazarev (also known as A.S. Gruzinsky) in which he said, "One must not put a loaded rifle on the stage if no one is thinking of firing it."

The Exercise

Write a short scene and introduce two objects at the opening of the scene. Make sure one of the objects is used later in the scene, but leave the other object unused. Note that these objects will not be part of the descriptive content. For example, if the scene includes a description of a room and mentions a chair in the corner, you don't have to use the chair later because it is part of the setting description.

Let your scene sit overnight, then read it back the next day. Notice how the unused object lingers in the reader's mind in an unpleasant way. Once you're done, feel free to revise and edit out the unnecessary object, or add action in which it becomes significant.

Tips: Differentiating between what constitutes a necessary or unnecessary element can be tricky. In some cases, a knife that is mentioned may not need to be played later (for example, a knife might be mentioned in the context of one of the characters eating). In other cases, a chair that is mentioned will need to be played. A woman might carry a purse, but that doesn't mean she needs to retrieve anything from it, because most women carry purses. On the other hand, if she's carrying a file marked TOP SECRET, the reader expects to eventually be let in on the contents of the file.

Variations: Go through a story you've already written, and look for instances in which you included unnecessary or misleading elements.

Applications: The difference between excellence and mediocrity in storytelling often lies in the details. Chekhov's gun is one of the many details that could cause a story to lose credibility with readers. Therefore, checking your narrative for unnecessary or irrelevant elements will strengthen and improve your work.

6.7 Oh No He Didn't!

Plot twists, cliffhangers, and page-turners. Oh my! These are the sneaky techniques writers use to keep readers captivated. And we've all been there. *It's late, and I'm tired. After this chapter, I'm going to bed.* Then there's a cliffhanger—a shocking development in the story. *Forget sleep! I have to find out what happens next!*

Some writers are criticized for overusing these devices or for planting twists that are contrived or forced. A good plot twist or cliffhanger is natural to the story and doesn't feel like the writer strategically worked it in.

Some stories feature major twists in the middle of chapters. It's placing such a twist at the end of a chapter that turns it into a cliffhanger. Soap operas and television dramas are known, loved, and loathed for their application of these devices. It's how they hook viewers, and it's a way you can hook readers.

Each writer has to decide whether to use these techniques in storytelling. You might think they're too strategic or rob your story of its artfulness. Or maybe you like the exciting edge that a good twist or cliffhanger brings to a story.

The Exercise

Write an outline for a scene or chapter that ends on a cliffhanger. Approach the cliffhanger by building tension to the moment:

The bad guys are chasing the good guys and gaining on them. They're getting closer. One of the bad guys draws his gun, lifts it, cocks it, and aims it at our hero. He pulls the trigger. See you next week!

You can also plant a cliffhanger that comes out of nowhere. The chapter is winding down, everything is moving along as expected. Suddenly a character walks into a room and tells her ex-lover that she's pregnant—and he's the father. *Uh-oh!*

Both types of cliffhangers work equally well.

Tips: The best cliffhangers leave huge questions hanging in the air. Who did it? What just happened? Will they survive? How is that possible? What will happen next?

Variations: You can expand on this exercise by fleshing out a scene that ends on a cliffhanger (instead of outlining). To expand further, write the follow-up scene and satisfy the reader's curiosity by answering the big questions raised by your cliffhanger.

Applications: If you want to be a commercially successful author, you will probably find that mastering the cliffhanger is a huge asset to your writing skills. The cliffhanger is almost mandatory in horror and mystery genres, so if that's what you want to write, you'll need to be able to execute a good clincher.

6.8 Danger and Conflict

Lots of writers complain about the horrible things they must do to their characters. You create them and develop a special affection for them. They're practically your children. And you pretty much have to torture them.

Characters must suffer. Otherwise there's no sense of overcoming obstacles. There's nothing to resolve. That means there is no story.

There can't be a resolution if there is no conflict. Conflict is generally unpleasant. So unpleasant, in fact, that many writers are completely derailed from writing fiction because they can't stand hurting their characters.

Suffering is part of life. Great fiction mirrors life, which is why we so often hear that not only is truth stranger than fiction, fiction often holds greater truths than reality. When your characters agonize over their circumstances, they are tested. They might lose something (or someone), but they might gain something greater.

We could talk for days about clouds with silver linings and how it's darkest before the dawn. These clichés only serve to remind us that life is what we make of it. Sometimes, what is more important than the danger or conflict is how your character reacts to it. Consider the following scenarios in stories where parents lost a child:

- One father founds a nonprofit organization dedicated to finding missing children.

- One mother fights off depression for over a decade until she finally seeks help and learns to rebuild her life.

- One couple divorces. The husband sinks into alcoholism. The wife spins into self-destruction.

The way we react to a crisis is based on our personalities, philosophies, and the way we were raised. Keep this in mind as you rake your characters over the coals.

The Exercise

You can create a new character especially for this exercise or use a character you have already developed. Decide what is this character's greatest fear. Then make it happen by writing a riveting scene packed with tension and conflict.

Tips: If you can't think of something that would terrify your character, look up phobias on the web and make one of those phobias your character's biggest fear.

Variations: You can sketch a scenario instead of writing out the narrative. For example, a character with a mortal fear of drowning survives a helicopter crash that leaves him floating in the middle of the Pacific Ocean.

Applications: This is a basic tenet of storytelling. Anytime you write a story, there must be conflict. It's not always the character in a deathly situation or facing his or her greatest fear, but it is always unpleasant. In other words, if you can't make your characters suffer (or at least make them extremely uncomfortable), you're going to have a hard time writing stories that resonate with readers.

6.9 Plots

In his book *The Seven Basic Plots: Why We Tell Stories*, Christopher Booker claims that there are only seven different plots in all of storytelling.

Booker's argument sparked much discussion among writers and readers, and a great debate ensued. Is it true? Are there only seven plots? And if so, how could any story written after the first seven be original?

You can have a lot of fun trying to categorize your favorite fiction into one of Booker's seven plot categories:

1. Tragedy
2. Comedy
3. Overcoming the monster
4. Voyage and return

5. Quest

6. Rags to riches

7. Rebirth

Booker's concept of limited possibilities within fiction is not a new idea. Joseph Campbell dissected the major elements of narrative and produced the monomyth (or hero's journey) in *The Hero with a Thousand Faces*, which identified the core plot elements of successful storytelling (see exercise 6.2). Campbell's ideas have been applied, tested, dissected, rearranged, and resurrected by writers, filmmakers, and literary analysts.

Another common breakdown of plot boils them all down to three possibilities:

1. Man against man

2. Man against nature

3. Man against himself

And we wonder why it seems like everything's been done.

The Exercise

Choose ten stories that you have read. You may also use stories from film or television, but make sure at least half of your stories come from good old-fashioned books. You'll need a piece of paper (or electronic document) with three columns. List the story titles you've chosen in one column. In the second column, assign each of the stories to one of the three plots listed above (man vs. man, man vs. nature, man vs. himself). In the third column, assign one of

Christopher Booker's seven plots to each of the stories you've chosen.

Tips: The main plot centers around the core climax and resolution, which occurs at or near the end of a story. All other plots are subplots.

Variations: For this exercise, you are asked to identify the main plot. As an alternative or bonus exercise, you can also assign each subplot from a story to a plot type.

Applications: Plot and character are two of the core elements in any story. Therefore, every writer benefits from mastering these elements first as a reader, then as a writer. As a storyteller, you should be able to identify the different types of plots in any story you read or write. Additionally, many writers suffer from lack-of-originality syndrome. They feel that every idea they have has already been done, so why bother writing anything at all? This exercise shows you that there are no new ideas, but you should forge ahead anyway.

6.10 Subplots

Subplots enrich a story. They give it layers so that it feels more like real life.

Think about your life and the events happening around you at any moment in time. There is never just one thing happening. There are many things going on. Some of them are not related to each other; others are closely intertwined. That is the reality in which we all live. For a story to feel real, whether it's based on true events or is completely imagined, it must mimic the complexity of real life.

One story's subplot may be another story's main plot. In a romance novel, the main plot is about the two main characters coming together and falling in love. But subplots abound: problems at work, conflict with family, surviving a disaster. In another genre, the romance might be a subplot, while another plot takes the main stage. A story about a broken family trying to survive the aftermath of a tornado might include a subplot wherein one of the characters falls in love.

A story can have one or two subplots, or it can be dense with them. Some subplots occur in sequence: one after another. Others are woven throughout the entire narrative. A master writer can introduce a wide range of subplots to the extent that the reader often focuses on them, rather than on the main plot.

The Exercise

Start by coming up with a few characters and a main plot, which will span the entire length of your story. Now, decide how you can weave three to five subplots throughout the main plot. Write an outline and notes about how the plot and subplots will be intertwined. Building a timeline can also be helpful.

Tips: Many novels are structured so that there is one main plot plus several subplots. The subplots can be threaded through the story or they can occur in single chapters or scenes. Set up at least one of your subplots to reconcile in a single scene or chapter early in the story, and set up at least one that will thread to the end.

Variations: Practice identifying subplots in some of your favorite books and movies. Use the plot types listed in exercise 6.9 as guidelines.

Applications: When writing a story, there is a lot to manage. The more characters a story has, the more plots and subplots it will have. At times, a complex story can feel unmanageable. Practicing on a small scale will help you see how to keep elaborate stories, plots, and subplots organized.

Chapter 7: Form Poetry

Working within a framework

7.1 Couplets and Quatrains

Poetry may not be the most widely read or published form of writing these days, but it's probably the most widely written.

Despite the lack of enthusiasm for the form among readers and publishers, poetry still has a traditional place in our culture. You'll hear poetry read at most significant events, such as weddings, funerals, graduation ceremonies, and presidential inaugurations. Poetry is the foundation for most children's books, and it's so closely related to songwriting that in many cases, it's hard to tell the difference between a poem and a song lyric.

Couplets and quatrains are two of the most basic building blocks of poetry.

Couplets

A couplet is a pair of lines in a poem. The lines usually rhyme and have the same meter or syllable count. Contemporary couplets may not rhyme; some of them use a pause or white space where a rhyme would occur.

Couplets can be used in a number of ways. Some poems are simply a couplet. Other poems are composed of a series of couplets. Stanzas can end with a couplet, or an entire poem can end with a couplet.

Quatrains

A quatrain is either a four-line stanza within a poem or a poem that consists of four lines. Many modern song lyrics are composed of quatrains.

A quatrain may contain one or two couplets. The nursery rhyme "Humpty Dumpty" is a quatrain of two couplets:

> Humpty Dumpty sat on a wall,
> Humpty Dumpty had a great fall.
> All the king's horses and all the king's men
> Couldn't put Humpty together again.

The Exercise

This is a three-part exercise. First, write a couplet (two rhyming lines with the same meter or number of syllables). Then, write a quatrain (it doesn't have to include meter or rhymes). Finally, write a quatrain that consists of two couplets.

Tips: Keep your language and subject matter simple. Aim for catchy language and vivid imagery.

Variations: Mix it up—write a poem that consists of a couplet followed by a quatrain and then another couplet. Try using couplets and quatrains to write a song lyric.

Applications: Couplets and quatrains have an infinite number of practical applications for a writer. Couplets are ideal for writing a children's story, because kids gravitate to simple language and rhythmic rhymes. You can also use couplets and quatrains in songwriting and greeting-card poetry.

7.2 Iambic Pentameter

If you chat long enough with a poet, eventually this term is sure to pop up in the conversation. Iambic pentameter is, historically, the most common metrical line used both in poetic verse and in verse dramas.

An *iamb* is a type of meter (in poetry we call it a foot, which is a unit of poetic measurement). It is an unstressed syllable followed by a stressed syllable: da DUM. Words that are iambs include the following: conCERN, eVOLVE, aMEND, eLUDE, toDAY.

A *pentameter* is five units (or five feet).

Therefore, *iambic pentameter* is a line of verse that is five iambs:

da DUM da DUM da DUM da DUM da DUM

Iambic pentameter can be used throughout an entire poem or just in certain lines or stanzas. Here is a couplet written in iambic pentameter:

I walked across a meadow in the rain

I danced beneath a starry summer sky

Iambic pentameter can take on a singsong quality or a brooding tone. It's quite musical, and its emotional quality depends largely on the flavor of words and images used.

While not in heavy use nowadays, except in songwriting, iambic pentameter has been quite popular throughout history. William Shakespeare used it in his plays and sonnets.

The Exercise

Write a poem in iambic pentameter. It can be a short poem, but make it at least four to six lines long. The lines don't have to rhyme, but rhymes will give your poem a nice musical quality.

Tips: Pay special attention to the stressed syllables, remembering that the first syllable is unstressed and every alternating syllable after that is stressed.

Variations: Iambic tetrameter is four feet of iambs: da DUM da DUM da DUM da DUM. Iambic trimeter has three feet of iambs: da DUM da DUM da DUM. As you can imagine, iambic meter ranges from one to ten (or more) feet of iambs per line. Write a poem in one of the other iambic forms.

Applications: As with so many poetic forms, iambic pentameter is ideal for children's stories and verses. It's also a useful tool in songwriting.

7.3 The Sonnet

The sonnet is the most well-known poetry form, largely because the most famous English writer of all time, William Shakespeare, had a penchant for writing sonnets. That was about four hundred years ago.

Today's poets tend to prefer free-form poetry, often without any rhyme scheme or discernible pattern. So why should we study outdated forms like sonnets, and why should we experiment with them?

Sonnets, along with all other literary forms and genres, make up our collective literary history. It is beneficial for writers to be familiar with the literary canon, which is the foundation upon which the entire writing profession is built.

Writing in form (even if just for practice) provides rules and boundaries. If you can learn to write well within form, then you will write even better outside of it.

When you practice writing in form, you face a specific challenge within a framework. If you write an English sonnet, each of your lines must be ten syllables. While this sounds limiting, it provides boundaries that you can work within. Sometimes too much freedom is overwhelming. Most writers have felt intimidated by a blank page. Form provides a structure that often makes writing easier.

Form also allows a writer to expend more creative energy on a poem's content. There is much to balance when writing a poem—language, rhythm and meter, word choice, subject matter, imagery. With rhythm and meter out of the way, you can concentrate on other aspects of the poem.

What is a Sonnet?

A sonnet is a fourteen-line poem that follows a strict rhyme scheme and focuses on a single thought, idea, or emotion. Most sonnets are found in lyric poetry, which conveys personal feelings and is sometimes set to music.

English sonnets are among the most famous types of sonnets, thanks to William Shakespeare. He wrote 154 of them, which is why English sonnets are also sometimes called Shakespearean sonnets. They are fourteen lines, and each line consists of ten syllables written in iambic pentameter (see exercise 7.2 for more information on iambic pentameter). The structure of an English sonnet is a set of three quatrains (four-line stanzas) followed by a rhyming couplet (two lines). The final couplet usually summarizes the entire poem. The rhyme scheme is ABAB CDCD EFEF GG.

Below is an English sonnet written by Shakespeare, annotated to show the rhyme scheme. Keep in mind that English pronunciation back in the sixteenth and seventeenth centuries differed from today's pronunciation. When this poem was composed, words like *temperate* and *date* would have been spoken in strict rhyme.

Sonnet 18: "Shall I Compare Thee to a Summer's Day"

William Shakespeare

(A) Shall I compare thee to a summer's day?

(B) Thou art more lovely and more temperate.

(A) Rough winds do shake the darling buds of May,

(B) And summer's lease hath all too short a date.

(C) Sometime too hot the eye of heaven shines,

(D) And often is his gold complexion dimmed;

(C) And every fair from fair sometime declines,

(D) By chance, or nature's changing course untrimmed.

(E) But thy eternal summer shall not fade

(F) Nor lose possession of that fair thou ow'st;

(E) Nor shall death brag thou wand'rest in his shade,

(F) When in eternal lines to time thou grow'st,

(G) So long as men can breathe or eyes can see,

(G) So long lives this, and this gives life to thee.

The Exercise

Write an English sonnet.

Tips: Make sure your sonnet focuses on one theme, subject, or idea. Part of the appeal of a sonnet is its subject matter, which is usually personal or intimate. Also, double check your rhyme scheme and meter (syllable count).

Variations: While sonnets are all fourteen lines long, the structure varies. In addition to English sonnets, there are Italian sonnets, Occitan sonnets, Spenserian sonnets, and modern sonnets. Each of these sonnet forms sets forth structural rules; for example, the Italian sonnet includes an eight-line stanza (octave) followed by a six-line stanza (sestet). Additionally, there are variations within each group. You can find a host of sonnet forms by doing a quick search on the Internet. Spend some time studying these forms and experimenting with them.

Applications: Many literary journals and poetry magazines accept poems for submission, and most will welcome a sonnet.

7.4 Haiku

Although haiku appears to be one of the simplest poetry forms, it's actually quite complex. To truly understand haiku, you need to know a little bit about the Japanese language, or more specifically, some key differences between Japanese and English. Also, traditional haiku adhere to strict rules regarding form and content.

A haiku consists of seventeen *mora*s or phonetic units. The word mora can be loosely translated as *syllable*.

A haiku is a seventeen-syllable verse. Traditionally, haiku were written on a single line, but modern haiku occupy three lines of 5-7-5 syllables.

Haiku also use a device called *kireji* (cutting word). This word breaks the haiku into two parts that are distinctly different but inherently connected. The kireji is not a concept used in English, so poets writing haiku in English often use punctuation marks instead of kireji, usually a hyphen or ellipsis.

The kireji provides structure to the verse and emphasizes imagery used on either side. It may not always be easy to identify the kireji in a haiku, but if you look for a word or punctuation mark that abruptly breaks the train of thought and severs the haiku into two parts, you've probably found it.

Another basic element of haiku is the *kigo* (season word). A true haiku is set in a particular season and is fundamentally concerned with nature. The kigo might be an obvious word like *snow* (indicating winter), or it could be vague as with a word like *leaves* (which can be present in any season).

Contemporary Haiku

There is much debate (and some controversy) over what technically qualifies as a haiku. Some poets merely adhere to the 5-7-5 syllabic and line structure and disregard the kireji and kigo elements. Purists insist that a poem is not haiku if it does not meet all of the traditional requirements.

Additionally, many modern poets do not write haiku that exclusively focus on nature. Contemporary haiku explore just about any subject imaginable.

The Exercise

Try your hand at writing a few haiku. For this exercise, focus on writing a poem that is seventeen syllables on three lines with the following meter: 5-7-5.

Tips: The most captivating haiku are quite lovely and use imagery that is almost tangible. Many haiku have an element of surprise or use turns of phrase that are clever, reminiscent of puns.

Variations: Write a few haiku that follow stricter, more traditional rules. These haiku are concerned with nature and include the kireji (cutting word) and kigo (season word).

Applications: Haiku remain popular and can be found in literary and poetry journals. They are also ideal for social media (especially Twitter) and are fun and quick to write. They promote clear, concise writing and can help you cultivate the art of using vivid imagery.

7.5 The Double Dactyl

It sounds dangerous and threatening, but the double dactyl is actually harmless.

A dactyl is a trisyllabic metrical foot composed of one stressed syllable followed by two unstressed syllables. That sounds confusing, but just think of a dactyl as a three-syllable word or phrase in which the first syllable is stressed. The word *poetry* (*PO-et-ry*) is a dactyl. So are the words *blueberry* (*BLUE-ber-ry*) and *fantasy* (*FAN-ta-sy*).

A double dactyl is exactly what it sounds like: two consecutive dactyls. Therefore, *blueberry fantasy* is a double dactyl.

However, the term double dactyl also refers to a form of verse poetry. In informal settings, it might be referred to as *higgledy piggledy*, which is itself a double dactyl.

A double dactyl poem has two stanzas. Each stanza has three lines of double dactyls and a fourth line that includes one dactyl plus a single-syllable accented word. The fourth lines might be something like *blueberry pie* or *fantasy sky*. Here are a few more specifications:

- The last lines of the two stanzas have to rhyme with each other.

- The first line of the first stanza is nonsense. For example, *higgledy piggledy*.

- The second line in the first stanza is the poem's main subject and should be a proper noun and a double dactyl. For example, *President Washington*.

- At least one line in the second stanza has to be a single six-syllable word that is a double dactyl. For example, *agoraphobia*.

Originally, there was also a rule that any six-syllable word used in a double dactyl should never be used again in the same poem.

Because the rules are so detailed and specific, double dactyls are challenging to write, but they are also a lot of fun, and children love them because they are silly.

The Exercise

Write a double-dactyl poem.

Tips: There is a template you can use on the following page.

Variations: As an alternative, try to come up with a list of ten words that are dactyls and ten words or phrases that are double dactyls. Finally, come up with five proper nouns (names) that are double dactyls. After that, you might be more inclined (and prepared) to write a double-dactyl poem.

Applications: There will be times when you're writing and need to make words or sentences fit a certain space or rhythm. Writing form poems like double dactyls helps you build skills for such tasks. They also make great children's poems.

Double-Dactyl Poem Template

LINE		STANZA
1	Double-dactyl nonsense	First stanza
2	Double-dactyl proper noun and subject of poem	
3	Double dactyl	
4	One dactyl plus a single-syllable accented word	
5	Double dactyl	Second stanza
6	Double dactyl	
7	Double dactyl	Use at least one six-syllable word that is a double dactyl in any line of the second stanza.
8	One dactyl plus a single-syllable accented word; must rhyme with final line in first stanza	

7.6 Get Your Writing in Shape: The Lanterne

Shape writing is a fun exercise in fitting words into a defined space.

Like haiku, the lanterne form of poetry is from Japan. In this form, we write a poem that has a distinct shape—the shape of a Japanese lantern.

A lanterne has five lines. The first line consists of one syllable. The second line contains two syllables. The third line contains three syllables. The fourth line contains four syllables. The fifth line is a single syllable: (1-2-3-4-1). Each line must be able to stand on its own, so words and ideas cannot be started on one line and completed on the following line.

Some lanternes use a title to form a sixth line, which also functions as part of the poem.

One

dancing

in a crowd

people moving

still

Sometimes, poems accidentally form a shape. Poets may also intentionally fit a poem into a shape that is related to the poem's subject or provides extra insight to the poem.

The Exercise

Write a lanterne.

Tips: The ideas in each line can be connected but they also have to stand alone as separate ideas.

Variations: Pick some other shape and write a poem to fill it. Make sure you type it to see how it looks in print.

Applications: Writing a predetermined number of words, characters, or writing to fill a specific allotment of space is an excellent skill for any writer to possess. Sometimes you'll use these skills in poetry, fiction, and other forms of prose or narrative. If you're editing a paragraph with sentences that are all roughly the same length, you may need to create some rhythmic balance, so you'll want to revise some sentences to make them shorter, which is essentially the same as writing to a specific word or syllable count. If you write copy for a newspaper or magazine, you will often be given a space limitation.

7.7 Doggerel

Poets have a special term for poetry they find distasteful or unrefined. A doggerel is a poem that is considered to have little literary value. If a poem is called doggerel, it's basically being referred to as trash.

Doggerel breaches the rules of refined poetry; sometimes it does this intentionally. Poems that are dripping with sentiment to the point of preciousness are doggerel. So are poems that contain clichés. If the meter is broken, it's doggerel. If a haiku fails to meet the standards of the form, it could be considered doggerel. Other violations that mark a poem as doggerel include misordering words to fit a metrical or rhyme scheme, writing about a trivial or shallow subject, or handling subject matter ungraciously or poorly.

Doggerel is usually the result of incompetence on the part of the poet. However, doggerel is not just a word we use to label bad poems. Some poets intentionally write doggerel, and in doing so, they turn their noses up at sophisticated or academic poetry. These rascally poets breach the conventions of good poetry writing, thus creating doggerel, but they do this by writing poems that are witty, clever, and entertaining. One such application of doggerel would be to use it for a parody piece.

They say that to become a great writer, you first must write badly. Nobody knows for sure who "they" are or why "they" seem to know everything about everything, but "they" are usually right. So for this exercise, you're going to try to be bad.

The Exercise

Write a doggerel. Your poem should be at least eight lines long, and it should contain at least three of the following poetic violations: overbearing sentimentality, clichés, broken meter, bad rhymes, misplaced or disarranged words to make the lines fit the meter or rhyme scheme, and trivial subject matter.

Tips: Make your poem as bad as possible, and when you're done, have a good laugh at yourself.

Variations: If doggerel comes easily to you, then write a doggerel that parodies a famous work (a story, poem, or other piece of art) or a doggerel that is satirical.

Applications: Writing is rather serious business, unless you're a comedian, which most of us are not, especially those of us perusing books of creative writing exercises. Sometimes we need to lighten up a little and remember not to take ourselves too seriously. This exercise should help you do that.

7.8 Found Poetry

Writers worry too much about being original. They write a poem and throw it away, because some other poet already has already done the subject justice. They write a story and crumple it up, because the premise or the plot have been done before. Characters are too familiar. Stories are too formulaic. The words have all been used too many times.

Tue originality isn't about making something new. It's about taking what's out there and seeing it from a new perspective or combining existing ideas in fresh ways.

That's what found poetry is all about. You take an existing text and mold it into a poem. It's a collage with words instead of pictures. A found poem follows these rules:

- It is made up exclusively of existing texts.

- The words are not changed.

- There are few additions or omissions.

- Line breaks are imposed by the poet.

- The poet may work the text into a form.

They are called "found poems" because they are discovered rather than made. Surely, you've read a passage in a textbook or newspaper article and thought that there was a poem in there somewhere. Well, you just found a poem!

The best source texts for found poems come from prose that is not meant to be poetic: speeches, news articles, and textbooks. However, found poems can come from other poems, song lyrics, and stories. Lots of stories probably have poems hidden within.

The Exercise

This exercise might prove to be a bit of a treasure hunt. Peruse some source material in search of a hidden poem. Flip through newspapers and textbooks, or search online for texts of speeches, reports, and official documents. As you read through your source material, look for interesting images and metaphors or compelling language—words that pop. Keep the original text mostly intact, using line breaks and spacing to convert it into a poem. Go light on making changes, additions, and omissions.

Tips: A good place to start your search would be the Internet, because you can easily copy and paste the original text into a document and then work with it. Wikipedia is packed with articles on almost every subject imaginable. Search there for topics that interest you; it's a great resource for this exercise.

Variations: As you can imagine, poets like to break the rules and get creative. Some poets mix different texts together, changing and adding words and lines as they see fit. You can, too. You might also nestle some found poetry into a larger poem that you're writing.

Applications: The main purpose of this exercise is to promote creativity and learn how to turn something old into something new. This exercise also shows you how to see existing texts in new ways.

7.9 Serious Form: Rondeau, Rondel, Rondelet

Some poets refuse to write in form; they see it as old-fashioned or limiting. But others swear by form, insisting that within form, there is actually more room for creative thinking to blossom.

Your position on the matter should only be decided after you've experimented wholeheartedly with a variety of forms.

Most studious young and new poets throughout history have had to write in form before they were given a blank page and invited to try their hands at free verse. This is in keeping with tradition in studying the arts. A young singer who is not a songwriter doesn't get her own songs; she sings someone else's. A young painter first copies the masterpieces, then makes his own. Poetry is no different.

Let's look quickly at three different forms, all hailing from France.

Rondeau

A rondeau is fifteen lines long. It has three stanzas: a quintet (five lines), a quatrain (four lines), and a sestet (six lines), with the following rhyme scheme: AABBA AABR AABBAR. Note that R stands for refrain, which is a repetition. In the rondeau, the refrain is a short phrase taken from line one and repeated on lines eight and fifteen. Every line other than the refrains should have the same meter.

Rondel

A rondel is thirteen lines. It has two quatrains (four lines each) and a quintet (five lines), with the following rhyme scheme: ABba abAB abbaA. All the capital letters indicate refrains, which are repeated lines.

Rondelet

A rondelet consists of a septet (seven lines) with two rhymes and a refrain: AbAabbA (capital letters indicate refrains). The refrain is four syllables (tetrasyllabic) and all other lines are twice as long: eight syllables (octosyllabic).

The Exercise

Write a rondeau, rondel, or rondelet.

Tips: Before you begin, prepare your document by marking off the rhyme scheme and stanzas. See exercise 7.5 for an example showing how to construct a form poetry template. Make notes where you'll have to count syllables and place refrains. Stick to the form you choose, and focus on tight, concise word choices. Avoid any unnecessary or superfluous words. Also, search online for any of these three poetry forms and you'll find plenty of rondeaus, rondels, and rondelets that you can use as examples.

Variations: Instead of choosing one of these forms, write one poem in each of these forms. That way, you get more for your money (three writing exercises in one!).

Applications: There are many literary publications that accept form poetry. You may be able to get your rondeau, rondel, or rondelet published.

7.10 Invention of Form

Who came up with the sonnet or the haiku? How did certain forms of poetry become so popular? Why are some forms so unpopular? And how many forms have been left by the wayside, ignored by poets?

Here's a more interesting question: how would you like to become an inventor?

The Exercise

Invent your own form of poetry. The form you develop should have all of the following guidelines:

- How many total lines will the poem have?

- How many stanzas?

- How many lines in each stanza?

- How many syllables should the lines have?

- What is the rhyme scheme?

- Will any lines be repeated as refrains?

Finally, give the form a name and write a poem in it.

Tips: To approach the exercise tactically, create a template for your poem (see exercise 7.5 for a template example).

Variations: You can always combine two (or more) other forms. What if a form started with a haiku followed by quatrain? Think about ways you can combine and tweak existing forms.

Applications: While existing forms of poetry are useful for creating a framework in which you can make poems, developing your own form gives you practice at building your own structure.

Chapter 8: Free Verse

Language and literary devices

8.1 Growing Vocabulary

A writer's vocabulary is paramount. Yet many writers use the same commonplace words over and over again. Repetition is rampant in writing, even though we have a vast language full of interesting and meaningful words at our disposal.

There's no excuse for using weak and tired words. After all, tools like the thesaurus and dictionary are easy to use and freely available on the Internet.

Writers often focus on technical elements of the craft, such as grammar, spelling, and punctuation. We also spend a lot of time thinking about structure, setting, plot, and characters. However, word choice is what makes our writing distinct. It's where we develop a voice and how we take a line drawing and fill it with color. When your vocabulary is robust, your writing shimmers.

Word choice can mean the difference between a decent piece of writing and a fantastic piece of writing.

The Exercise

For this exercise, you'll need the following:

- a poem (this can be a poem you wrote or a poem by another author)

- writing tools (word processing software or pen and paper)

- a thesaurus

You can do this exercise on paper or electronically, but you'll need to make copies of the poem you've chosen to work with. An electronic format will be easier, since you can copy and paste with relative ease.

Step One: Nouns and Verbs

Go through the poem and highlight all the nouns and verbs. You can use bold, underlining, or italics. When you're done, work through the poem and replace each noun and verb with another word that has the same meaning. Try to pull replacement words from your mind, but don't wait too long before turning to the thesaurus. Double-check the dictionary definitions of words you pull from the thesaurus to ensure they have connotations that communicate your intent. When you're done, read the original and your revised poem. How do they differ?

Step Two: Adjectives and Adverbs

You'll need a fresh copy of the original poem. This time, go through and highlight all the adjectives and adverbs. Highlight entire phrases if necessary. When you're done, go through and replace each adjective and adverb with a word that has almost the same meaning but a slightly different connotation (for example, *green* becomes *mint*). Try to come up with replacement words on your own, but if you get stuck, use the thesaurus. When you're done, read the original and your revised poem. Did you succeed in creating a completely different poem by slightly changing the adjectives and adverbs? How are the two poems still alike?

Step Three: Double Up

Start over with two fresh copies of the original poem or two copies of another poem. First, highlight all the nouns, verbs, adjectives, and adverbs. Go through and replace all of these words with different words but try to keep the meaning, imagery, and general themes of the poem exactly the same.

Then go through the second copy of the same poem, but this time use words that have the same meaning but different connotations. Again, use the thesaurus, even if only to check your word choices. Did you successfully create one new poem that has the same sensibility of the original and one that is different?

Tips: After you've replaced words in a poem, use the new poem you've created as your next starter piece. You'll end up with a chain of poems, each one leading to the next.

Variations: Highlight adjective-noun and adverb-verb combinations (such as *home office* or *lightly sleeping*) and replace them with single words (such as *den* or *dozing*).

Lengthen a poem by replacing single words with longer phrases. *Green* becomes *the color of grass.* How does this change the overall impact of the poem? Is it weaker? Are its images clearer?

Applications: The most important benefit to this exercise is expanding your vocabulary and promoting variety in the word choices you make. However, if you modify your starter poem enough, it could become a new poem, which you can submit and publish.

8.2 Alliteration and Assonance

Developing a vocabulary of poetry terms and literary devices will help you better understand the writing techniques and tools that are at your disposal. It may not occur to you that you can build rhythm by repeating consonant sounds. When you know the meaning of *alliteration*, then this idea is more likely to influence your work.

Poetry terms, such as *alliteration* and *assonance*, show us how clever, creative word arrangements add musicality to any piece of writing, making it more compelling and memorable. These terms and the concepts they represent apply to all types of writing, not just poetry.

Alliteration is the repetition of the initial consonant sounds of words in close proximity to one another. Examples of alliteration include *black and blue*, *we walk*, and *time after time*.

In some cases, alliteration is used to refer to any repeated consonant sounds, even if they don't occur at the beginning of words. An example of this would be "blue notebook," where the *b* sound is repeated at the beginning of *blue* and in the middle of *notebook*.

Alliteration might also be used to describe the repetition of a consonant sound nestled in the middle or even at the end of words. *Blueberry*, for example, contains alliteration within a single word.

Assonance is similar to alliteration, except it deals exclusively with vowel sounds. Assonance occurs when accented vowel sounds are repeated in proximity:

Assonance allows literary writers to create fun phrases.

In the example phrase above, there are several runs of assonance. The opening *a* sounds in the words <u>*assonance*</u> and <u>*allows*</u> demonstrate one *run* of assonance. This run is marked with underlining. A second run is marked with bold lettering and occurs with the *a* sounds in **create** and **phrases**. Can you find a third run of assonance in the sentence?

Assonance often evokes a sense of rhyme without serving up a direct or technical rhyme. The phrase "fancy pants" is an example of this.

So, how are alliteration and assonance used for effect? Well, think about repetition in general. When you repeat something over and over, it becomes embedded in memory. Alliteration and assonance work the same way. If used correctly, these devices enhance the rhythm of a piece, making it more memorable.

The Exercise

Go through a piece of writing (your own or someone else's) and look for instances of assonance and alliteration.

The material you work with can be poetry, fiction, a journal entry, or a blog post. Any form of writing will do.

Mark the runs of assonance and alliteration with bold, underlining, italics, or highlighting. When you're done, read the piece aloud to get the full effect.

Tips: Double-check the runs you've identified for assonance to make sure they mark stressed (or accented) syllables. Watch out for sounds that are different but use the same letter (such as the *a* sounds in *cat* and *cape*).

Variations: As an alternative to identifying alliteration and assonance in a piece of writing, try writing a short piece with several runs in it. Or revise a page from an existing writing project to inject alliteration and assonance into it.

Applications: Musicality and repetition enrich any piece of writing. Too often, writers focus on content and not language. The study of poetry, poetry terms, and literary devices like alliteration and assonance reminds us to work on our language, word choice, and sentence structure.

8.3 Rock and Rhyme

Rhyming poetry goes in and out of vogue all the time, except when it comes to children's poetry, which is almost always packed with fun and clever rhymes.

Some poets take to rhyming rather easily, and soundalike words roll off their tongues like butter. Other poets struggle, dancing through the alphabet and flipping through rhyming dictionaries just to find a rhyme as simple as *bat* and *cat.*

Poems that rhyme are fun to write and a blast to read. They are especially fun to read out loud. Rhyming is good practice for exploring musicality in language and experimenting with wordplay.

The Exercise

All you need is a song—a rhythmic and rhyme-y song without a lot of fancy runs. You'll want a relatively simple tune. A short pop song will work well. Forget about classical music because most of it doesn't have lyrics, and what we're doing requires words. We're writers, right?

Rewrite the lyrics but keep the rhythm and rhyme scheme intact. You don't have to replace the rhyme *ring* and *sing* with a rhyme like *thing* and *bling.* But you do need to find another rhyming pair (like *dance* and *pants*). Your rhymes can be as strict or as loose as you want.

If you do just a few of these, rhyming will start to come more naturally to you, and your rhymes will flow with greater ease.

Try to rewrite the song on your own, but if you're really struggling, visit a rhyming dictionary or a thesaurus.

Tips: You might want to start with a short, three-chord pop song and then move on to longer and more complex tunes. If you know all the lyrics to your song, that will be immensely helpful. If not, do an online search to find the lyrics to the song you want to work with.

Variations: Here are a few variations that you can use for this exercise:

- Try it with nursery rhymes: "Hickory Dickory Dock."

- Try it with a famous poem. Shakespeare anyone?

- Try it using a song without lyrics. You're on your own!

Applications: Working with rhyme helps you think more carefully about word choice and points your focus to the sound and rhythm of a piece of writing. This is also an excellent exercise for anyone who has thought about writing song lyrics or children's poems and stories.

8.4 Show, Don't Tell: Imagery

Writers are often told *show, don't tell.* At first, it's a confusing piece of advice. Show what? Isn't writing all about telling readers something?

Yes and no.

When you tell readers that a couple walked hand in hand through the city streets, the image is bland. But when you say that a tall bearded man wearing a top hat and a trench coat and a small dark-haired woman in a red velvet gown walked hand in hand through deserted back alleys of a big city, a more vivid image enters the reader's mind. That's what we mean by *show, don't tell*. Imagery paints a picture.

Imagery is especially important in poetry because poetry often deals with the abstract: ideas, emotions, and themes. Wrangling these concepts into images isn't always easy, but the payoff is enormous.

Let's say you want to write a poem about injustice. You can tell readers some statistics about how many convicted criminals have been declared innocent thanks to DNA testing, or you could show them injustice by describing a man wrongfully convicted of murder and sentenced to death. Show this man as he eats his last meal, makes his last phone call, and faces his executioner. Finally, depict the real murderer, who is watching all of this on TV. This is how you show readers what you want to say instead of telling them.

The Exercise

To begin, think of a broad subject that you'd like to explore in a poem: love, hate, revenge, sacrifice, redemption, rebirth, time. Write a poem using imagery to depict what you want to say about this concept.

Tips: Imagery is part storytelling, part description, and part metaphor. Use images that are concrete and easy for readers to visualize. Try to avoid emotional language and instead focus on painting a picture through description.

Variations: As an alternative, go through some poems and identify the imagery that poets have used to convey a message or idea. Write your response to these images, and in your own words, explain why an image makes a poem's theme and concept more vivid.

Applications: Imagery strengthens every form of writing from storytelling and poetry to journal writing and journalism. It is one of the most powerful tools of the craft.

8.5 Cut-and-Paste Poetry

Most poetry-writing exercises are designed to help you focus on one particular area of poetry writing, such as rhyme, alliteration, or imagery. This one works on several levels.

First, this exercise provides a nice, Zenlike break from your daily routine, because it involves more than writing. You'll get to search through clippings and do a little cutting and pasting (the old-fashioned cutting and pasting with scissors and glue, not the computer-based cut and paste).

Second, this exercise provides an excellent alternative to recycling those growing stacks of old magazines, newspapers, and brochures that are sitting around collecting dust.

You can come back to this exercise again and again for future poetry writing sessions.

You'll need some supplies and some time. Try to set aside an hour or two (and note that you can break this exercise up over several days or even longer).

What You'll Need (Supplies)

- old printed material: magazines, newspapers, pamphlets, ads, photocopies, junk mail, etc.;

- a small box, basket, jar, or other container;

- a pair of scissors;

- a glue stick or a roll of clear tape;

- a piece of blank paper (construction paper works well; you can also use a piece of cardboard or a page in your notebook); and

- a highlighter (optional).

The Exercise

Step One: Go through old magazines, pamphlets, printouts, and photocopies. Any printed material will do. Scan through the text to find words and phrases that are interesting and capture your attention and imagination. You can highlight the text you like or move ahead to step two.

Step Two: Cut out the phrases you've chosen, and place them in your container.

Step Three: When you have a nice pile of clippings, pull some out and spread them across a flat work surface. Sift through the words, pairing different clippings together to see how the phrasing sounds. Place the ones you like best on a piece of paper, arrange them into a poem, and use glue or tape to adhere them.

Tips: Look for words and images that pop. When you're all done, save the leftover clippings so you can repeat this exercise again later.

Variations: If you find it difficult to cobble together an entire poem from your clippings, then use a pen or pencil to add words and phrases to complete your poem. You can also clip images and incorporate them to create a multimedia poetry collage that is also a piece of art.

Applications: This exercise reminds you to focus on word choice and language. It encourages you to go outside yourself for inspiration by piecing elements from different sources together to make something new.

8.6 Metaphor and Simile

Metaphor is an excellent tool for breathing life into your writing by engaging readers' senses and firing up their imaginations.

Metaphors fall somewhere between symbols and similes. A symbol is something that represents something else. It can be a word, a sign, or an image. Close your fist and extend your forefinger and middle finger into a V-shape. That's the symbol for peace (or victory, depending on the context).

A simile is when one thing is *like* another: Her skin was like snow: white and cold.

A metaphor, however, is when we say that one thing *is* another thing. Her skin is not like snow: it *is* snow. However, metaphors are not meant to be taken literally.

The most effective metaphors engage readers by connecting an otherwise intangible subject to a clear, concrete image or by triggering one (or more) of the five senses: sight, sound, smell, touch, or taste.

The Exercise

Choose a topic to write about. Some subjects don't need the help of a metaphor: sex, food, music, and anything else that intrinsically affects the senses will not benefit from a metaphor the way abstract topics will.

Next, choose a metaphor to represent your subject. The best metaphors are things that affect all the senses. Food is often used as a metaphor because it is multisensory: you can see, smell, touch, and taste it, and you can also hear it—food and drinks pop, fizz, sizzle, and splash.

Now that you have a topic and a metaphor to go with it, it's time to write a poem. Think about how you can extend the metaphor and weave it throughout your piece.

For example, you could use the metaphor of a fish in a poem about dancing. Think about the qualities of fish. They wiggle when they swim. They leap. They're slippery. They might make bubbles. How can you use the qualities of a fish to represent dancing?

Incorporate simile by expanding on your metaphor to include related words and images: water, boats, bait (the dancer is a fish, and the music is like bait).

Tips: Be careful not to overwhelm your piece with too many different metaphors or too much of the same metaphor. An overused metaphor gets tired, and too many different metaphors can be confusing. Aim for fresh metaphors and avoid clichés.

Variations: As an alternative, make a list of topics and match them with metaphors that would represent them well.

Applications: Think about subjects you've explored recently in your writing. Were there any ideas that felt flat or dry? You can revise those pieces using metaphor to add dimension and make your writing more compelling.

8.7 Concise Writing

Many modern poets argue that poetry is most effective when the language is condensed. That means eliminating extraneous or unnecessary words.

We writers tend to rely heavily on verbiage, especially modifiers (adjectives and adverbs) and articles (*a, an, the*) to add balance and rhythm to our writing or simply to make it sound smarter.

Language is the heart and soul of poetry. In any kind of writing, we need to think beyond the subject matter and pay due diligence to language and word choice. Poets are especially encouraged to search for the perfect words and phrases and to eliminate redundancy.

This exercise helps you look at your writing from a minimalist perspective. Simplify, and remember that less is more.

The Exercise

Step One: Remove Modifiers

Choose a poem (or other piece of writing) that you've already completed. Go through your poem and cross out all adjectives and adverbs. Take note of how many strikethroughs there are. Next, revisit your verbs and nouns, and see if you can replace them with alternative verbs and nouns that better reflect the image you were trying to convey when the modifiers were still in place.

Example: "The drooping tree" becomes "The ~~drooping~~ tree," which then becomes "The willow."

Step Two: Eliminate Articles

Continue with the poem you used in step one or start with a different piece. This time, go through and cross out all articles (*a, an, the,* etc.) Notice how many times these parts of speech appear in your piece. Now read it back without the articles. Does it sound better? Do you think you need to replace some of the articles for the poem to make sense?

Example: "~~The~~ old dresser sits in ~~the~~ corner" becomes "Old dresser sits in corner."

Step Three: No Excess

Now try the exercises again. This time, cross out the modifiers and the articles. Again, make note of how many strikethroughs you have. Read the poem aloud and see how it sounds. Better? Worse? Try replacing adjective-noun and adverb-verb combinations with nouns and verbs that are more descriptive (for example, *runs quickly* becomes *sprinted*). Do you need to put some of your modifiers and articles back into the piece? Were you able to find suitable and better replacements for the words you eliminated?

Example: "A bad dream haunts the young man" becomes "Nightmare haunts lad."

Tips: In working through this exercise, you will probably find that some modifiers and articles simply cannot be replaced. A chocolate chip cookie is not just any old cookie, and there is simply no other way to describe it clearly and effectively.

Variations: This exercise is ideal for groups or partners. Each person contributes a writing project, and then everyone swaps papers for the exercise.

Applications: This is an exercise in self-editing and learning how to cut extraneous and unnecessary words while replacing weak words with stronger, more compelling ones.

8.8 Freewriting Harvest

In the first chapter of this book, we explored freewriting. Freewriting has a number of useful applications. It can help you clear your mind so you can focus on a writing project, it works as a problem-solving tool, and it promotes creativity.

Freewriting is also an excellent way to generate raw material for your writing projects.

This exercise shows you how to use freewriting to create and harvest raw material for your poetry.

The Exercise

If you haven't read chapter 1 or completed any freewriting exercises yet, go back and read through the chapter. It's short and should only take a couple of minutes to read or review. You should also do a few freewrites (feel free to spread them out over several days).

In freewriting, you write whatever comes to mind, no matter how silly, outrageous, or nonsensical. If your mind goes blank, just write the word *blank* over and over until something else comes to mind. You can jot down ideas, words, and images. Write for about twenty minutes.

If you've already done some freewriting exercises, then you can use one of them for this exercise.

Go through your freewrite and highlight words, phrases, and images that pop or capture your attention. These might be excerpts that have a musical quality or passages that inspire a vivid scene or image in your mind. You might highlight a single word that you find interesting, or you might highlight an entire passage that is a few lines long.

When you've finished making your highlights, extract the highlighted portions of text. Either rewrite these sections on a fresh page in your notebook or copy and paste them into a new document. Now, you've harvested your freewrite for raw material and are ready to start building a poem.

Using the material you've harvested, add and remove words and phrases. Rethink the line breaks. Try to work it into a form (if you wish) or arrange the poem so that it flows rhythmically.

Tips: The more you freewrite, the more raw material you will generate. Try freewriting for twenty minutes a day for five days during the week, and then spend the weekend making poems out of your raw material.

Variations: You can go through several freewrites at a time. One freewrite might lead to three poems, or five freewrites might generate material that goes into a single poem. You can even harvest material from numerous freewrites into a new "freewrite remix" and then harvest that for your poetry material.

Applications: Many poets use freewriting to generate raw material. You will find that as you continue to freewrite on a regular basis, your freewriting sessions become more and more interesting (everything gets better with practice). Some freewrites might even translate directly into poems with very little revision necessary.

8.9 Twitter Poems

We're always changing and evolving. First we had the postal system, then the telegraph, followed by the telephone. Now, we're totally connected: cell phones, smart phones, video phones, and online chats.

Social media has changed the game in terms of how we write, where we write, and whom we engage with through written communications. The Internet demands that we become clearer and more concise.

Twitter has spawned a whole new generation of writing styles. Piggybacked on text-messaging shorthand (u no what i mean), Twitter insists that we communicate, share, and interact in 140 characters or fewer. That's a very small space to get any point across.

Yet it has proved to be a huge success. In the age of sound bites, Twitter fits nicely with all the blurbs, questions, and exclamations that we make in the public arena.

Writers have flocked to Twitter and found it tremendously useful in connecting with readers and other writers. Many have even developed new forms of writing around the 140-character limitation: Twitter stories and Twitter poems.

The Exercise

The exercise is short and simple: write a poem in 140 or fewer characters. If you can write exactly 140 characters, give yourself an extra pat on the back.

Tips: Haiku lends itself well to Twitter poetry. In fact, you can log onto Twitter and search for haiku (use hashtag #haiku).

Variations: Another popular trend online is the six-word story. You can invent your own forms (the eight-word poem, for example) and work them into the 140-character limitation.

Applications: The most obvious application is that you can post your poem (in its entirety) on Twitter. You can also write a series of short poems, or perhaps your 140-character poetry tweets can be strung together into a longer poem.

8.10 Word Prompts for Poetry

Sometimes poets run out of words. We get tired or busy. We get stressed out. We can't be inspired or full of ideas every day, but that's no excuse for not writing.

Writers often complain about writer's block, but it's quickly going out of fashion as an empty excuse for not writing. There are just too many sources of inspiration available to us, and we're living in a no-excuses age.

Writing prompts are one of the best ways to generate ideas when our muses are on strike. Some prompts present a quick premise, image, or scene. Others ask questions. Some are just simple lists of words that you can use to spark a writing session.

The Exercise

Below, you'll find several word lists. The first five lists are general and the other four lists are inspired by the seasons. Choose a list and write a poem using all the words in the list. Or choose a season list and write a poem about that season. Make sure you use every word from the list you choose.

One: bronze, forgotten, scratchy, dust, mount

Two: plastic, zealous, manipulate, charity, test

Three: velvet, opera, spin, collision, dance, slide

Four: pristine, highway, moth, skyline, curl, river

Five: terminal, check, wait, keys, silver, island, hatch

Spring: fresh, green, clean, shoot, seeds, hatchling

Summer: ball, bucket, ice, thunder, lemonade, tan

Fall: rake, squash, golden, harvest, feast, pumpkin, soup

Winter: blizzard, fire, skate, shiver, holiday, night

Tips: Look for words that have multiple meanings. For example, *rock* can mean a pebble or a boulder or it can indicate a genre of music. It can also be an action (rock the baby). Words with multiple meanings can add dimension to a poem.

Variations: The variations are limitless. You can mix and match words from different lists. You can put two or more lists together. You can also write a single poem with all the words from all the lists.

Applications: Writing prompts are lifesavers when you sit down to write and nothing happens. You can always use prompts for a writing session. Sometimes you'll get your best work this way. It may even be publishable!

Chapter 9: Philosophy, Critical Thinking, and Problem Solving

The importance of truth and reason

9.1 The Great Debate

Logic, order, and organization are essential in clear and coherent writing, whether you're telling a story or writing a poem. Critical thinking is a fundamental writing skill.

If a story doesn't stand up to logic, or if a poem has holes in its philosophy, readers will become disenchanted. If a character does something outrageous but doesn't have a reasonable motive, readers will become disengaged.

Writing requires foresight and analysis. We use what-if questions to create, and we use if-then arguments to substantiate everything we write.

We often think of arguments as conflicts, and most arguments are. A neighbor doesn't want to chip in for a fence that divides two properties, and an argument ensues. A spouse comes home late after forgetting to call. An argument ensues. A child comes home with a bad grade. Another argument.

Argument does not always stem from personal conflict. The greatest debates throughout history have dealt with philosophical issues—questions to which there are no absolute answers. While our characters will surely experience personal arguments, it is our mastery of the philosophical arguments that will make a narrative reasonable and believable.

The Exercise

First, you'll need to pick an issue or philosophical question (suggestions are provided below). Write a piece of dialogue between two speakers in which they engage in a debate, with each taking an opposing side in the argument. Write it as a simple script. Here are some topics to get you started:

- One speaker believes in a supreme being or higher power, and the other does not.

- Fate or free will? One believes in destiny, the other believes that life's outcome is strictly the result of choice and circumstance.

- Do good and evil exist? One believes good and evil are struggling to eradicate each other. Another argues that good and evil are relative, subjective, or mere human imaginings.

- Are morals and ethics circumstantial or static? One believes it's always wrong to kill another person, no matter the circumstance. The other believes in the death penalty or self-defense.

- One speaker believes in life after death, and the other believes it all just ends.

Another source of ideas for philosophical debates is political issues.

Tips: This exercise will work best if you pick an issue with which you're familiar but on the fence. For example, perhaps you know a lot about the death penalty but haven't taken a stance on it. Since you are not on either side, you will probably do a good job arguing for both sides. However, if you want to choose an issue that you feel strongly about, you should do your best to convey the opposing arguments in a convincing manner. You can also research any of these issues to get some ideas about positions on the matter.

Variations: As an alternative, you can write two short essays (one page each) for and against the issue you have chosen. You can also engage a friend to write an opposing viewpoint.

For an extra challenge, find a friend who truly disagrees with you on an issue, and write each other's arguments. See if you can present the other side's best positions and ideas, and then critique each other's papers.

Applications: You might have two characters in a story who have basic philosophical differences. Such opposition could split a tribe, end unity in a nation, or break up a relationship. Philosophical issues often arise as themes in storytelling, poetry, and journalism.

9.2 Facts in Fiction

We live in a world of sound bites. Everyone has an opinion, and "facts" are flung around carelessly without any consideration for their source or accuracy. There are entire websites dedicated to fact-checking major media outlets in an effort to quell the spread of misinformation.

In writing, when the facts don't jibe with what's happening on the page, readers get irritated and could be provoked to write a negative review. Writers end up looking foolish, because they failed to do a little research and fact checking, even within the context of their own story.

In chapter 1, you have a character who mentions that her mother will be angry if she chooses a particular college. Then, in chapter 10, we learn that character's mother has been in a coma since she was in junior high. So, it's not possible for her mother to have been angry about her choice of college, since she would have been unconscious at the time the college was chosen.

In a poem about war, you mention a battle but attach the wrong general or battalion to it.

Facts are even more important when you're writing nonfiction. If you fudge the facts or fail to do your research, your credibility suffers, and you could lose readers (and sales).

These kinds of mistakes make writers look bad. Readers have sharp memories. They are smart and educated. Do not underestimate them.

In this exercise, you'll learn to back up your claims with facts, even when you're writing fiction.

The Exercise

You'll need a piece of writing that you've already completed. The best pieces will be narrative (fiction or nonfiction) rather than poetry. If you've completed exercises earlier in this book, then you can use one of the stories you wrote. Go through the piece and do a fact check. Below are some examples of what to look for:

- Distances: If a family lives in California, and their child goes to college in New York but later embarks on a two-hour drive home for the holidays, you need to fix the facts.

- Time: If a character is twenty years old in 2010 and mentions seeing *Saturday Night Fever* at the theater when it first came out, you have a problem because the movie came out before he was born.

- Science and technology: Make sure your gadgets and devices exist in the time frame in which you're writing. Also, check facts that relate to science. For example, if your story is set on a planet with two moons, you should conduct research to find out how two moons will affect the tides and other natural phenomenon.

- History: Research is absolutely essential when you're writing historical fiction. However, even in contemporary fiction, there may be references to the past. If a character's aunt danced with Elvis, make sure the ages of the characters in the story align with Elvis's life, and make sure the dance didn't happen when Elvis was overseas.

- Props and costumes: Be aware of what characters are wearing and the settings they are in. If a character puts on tennis shoes before leaving the house, she can't lose a heel trying to climb into her car.

Tips: Checking facts in fiction can be difficult. As we read our own work, we might be more inclined to revise the language or look for typos than to question factual accuracy. One tool you can use is a timeline, which comes in handy when checking for accuracy in your timeline. Find friendly, knowledgeable readers who can review your work to check for fallacies and inaccuracies.

Variations: If you don't have a piece of writing that works with this exercise, do an observation exercise instead. The website moviemistakes.com lists mistakes that have been found in films. Some of these are continuity errors rather than factual errors (for example, in a single scene, an actor's hair is wet in one shot, dry in the next). Choose a movie, but don't look at the list of mistakes. Watch the movie, and look for the mistakes. Write a list of all the mistakes you observe. Then, check the list to see how many you found. Did you discover any new mistakes? How many did you miss?

Applications: Don't distract your readers by failing to align your facts, and don't damage your credibility as an author by forgetting to conduct proper research. The fact that a website called Movie Mistakes exists is a testament to the keen observational skills that fans, including moviegoers and readers, possess and the degrees to which they will go to publicize an artist's failure to get the facts right.

9.3 Everyone Has an Opinion

All good pieces of writing have a central conflict. The entire narrative builds up to the moment when the conflict reaches its final climax.

In addition to a central conflict, several smaller conflicts along the way build tension.

One way to create light conflict is through opposing opinions. After all, everybody has an opinion, and we constantly disagree with each other. That doesn't mean we're always fighting, but it does mean there is a bit of abrasion in our daily dealings.

Real people think differently from one another and so must characters. Think about your favorite books, movies, TV shows, and music. Do your friends and family all agree with you on who should have won last year's award for best new artist? Of course not. It's unlikely that everyone you know belongs to the same political party, attends the same church, or even favors the same restaurants.

Opinions and personal beliefs often seem unimportant, but sometimes they affect the course of events. Here's a scenario:

> Someone breaks in to a chemical plant and is tinkering with the equipment. The two guards on duty apprehend the suspect, who turns out to be a former employee. He insists that there's a major chemical leak, which will cause a massive explosion, killing hundreds of nearby residents if they don't let him fix it. One guard thinks the suspect is telling the truth. But the other guard believes he is lying and is actually trying to set off the explosion rather than render it inert. Neither knows for sure, and the clock is ticking.

The entire scene balances on these two characters' opinions about the third character. Which guard will win the argument?

Characters might engage in debates over anything—from which superhero can run the fastest to whether or not there is an afterlife.

The Exercise

Nothing makes your characters seem real like giving them their own beliefs and opinions. From which fast-food restaurant has the best fries to who was the greatest leader in history, character opinions can run the gamut.

Write a scene in which characters reveal their opinions about a variety of things. Include three (or more) characters and at least six different opinions (two for each character) through the course of the scene. Try to reveal one insignificant opinion and one serious belief for each character.

Tips: Write a scene that flows smoothly. Don't make it obvious that the point of the scene is to reveal the characters' opinions and beliefs. To do this, you'll need to develop a context in which the scene takes place: a court hearing, a classroom, or a newsroom are all settings where debate might arise.

Variations: If you're already working on a narrative writing project, then feel free to engage in this exercise within that project. Work the characters' opinions into the conversation in an existing scene or in the next scene you write.

Applications: This exercise gets you thinking about your characters in new ways. What do they think or believe about insignificant and important matters? It also requires you to create smaller conflicts, instead of relying solely on a central conflict. This adds depth, complexity, and realism to your writing.

9.4 *Moral Dilemmas*

It's not enough for your characters to have simple opinions. Each of us also has deeper philosophical ideals and values. Our values come from our families, religions, and cultures. They shape our morals and the decisions we make.

People are complex. What we believe is right or wrong changes when we find ourselves in real situations. Consider an honorable character who believes that one's highest loyalty is to his or her family. When that character learns her brother is a serial killer, does she turn him in? Testify against him? Stories get interesting when characters' morals are put to the test.

The Exercise

For this exercise you will put a character's morals to the test. Below, you'll find a short list of moral dilemmas. Write a scene in which a character faces one of these moral dilemmas and has to make an agonizing decision.

- In the novel *Sophie's Choice*, a young Polish mother and her two children are taken to a concentration camp. Upon arrival, she is forced to choose one child to live and one to die. If she doesn't choose, they both die. Write a scene in which your character must choose between the lives of two loved ones.

- A single woman is close friends with the couple next door and has secret romantic feelings for the husband. She discovers his wife is having an affair. Normally, this woman minds her own business, but now she sees an opportunity to get closer to the man she wants.

- Some countries have strict laws regarding drug possession. A family has traveled to one such country for vacation. Upon arrival (or departure), one of the teenager's bags is sniffed out by a dog. The bag is opened, the drugs are identified, and the guard asks whose bag it is. Both parents are considering claiming ownership. Everyone in the family knows the sentence would be death.

- Travel through time and face this classic moral dilemma: The protagonist is holding a loaded gun, alone in a room with a two-year-old baby Hitler.

- A plane crashes into the sea. Most of the passengers escape with inflatable lifeboats but they do not board them correctly. Your character ends up on a lifeboat that holds eight people, but there are twelve people on it, and it's sinking. Your character can either throw four people overboard and eight will survive, or they will all die except your character, who will get rescued after the others drown.

During the scene, the character should agonize over the decision and reveal his or her reasons for the choice he or she makes.

Tips: Search online for "lists of moral dilemmas" to get more scenarios.

Variations: If you don't want to write a scene, challenge yourself to come up with a few moral dilemmas of your own.

Applications: These moral dilemmas also work as story prompts. They force you to put your characters in situations that are deeply distressing, thus creating conflict and tension.

9.5 Chain of Events

One could argue that every event in the universe, from the earth-shattering explosion of an A-bomb to a little leaf fluttering in the breeze, is part of a long chain of events.

For every action, there's a reaction. A chirping bird outside someone's window could keep him up all night, and he could get into a car accident the next day after falling asleep at the wheel. That car accident could be fatal to a passenger in another car. The death of that passenger brings on severe depression in one of his or her loved ones. That person seeks therapy. While in the waiting room, he or she meets an attractive stranger. They end up getting married, and it all started with a chirping bird.

If you think hard and long about how every little thing in the universe is connected, your mind might become overwhelmed, so let's keep it simple.

The Exercise

Start with an event. It could be something major, like a group of revolutionaries attacking a military command center, or it could be something minor, like a woman leaving her house and going to the store to buy milk late at night. Start with that event and then work backward, listing all the other little actions and events that led up to it. Try to go fifteen to twenty steps back. If you're working on a story or some other writing project, you can use an event or incident from your story. Working backward this way will help you see your narrative and plot in a new light.

When you're done, come back to the event you started with and work forward. Again, take fifteen to twenty steps in the timeline.

Your chains don't have to be too complicated. You're not writing a story, you're just exploring how events and actions are linked together in a chain.

Tips: In reality, events are not the result of a single-link chain of events. It's more like a chain-link fence.

Multiple things might happen to cause a woman to run out and buy milk late at night: she had a full container of milk but left it out overnight, and it spoiled. Then she lost her shopping list when she went to the grocery store, so she forgot to buy more. It's late; her husband and kids are sleeping, but she knows the baby will wake up in the middle of the night and need a bottle. Multiple events conspired to cause her to go out at night for some milk.

Variations: If you really want to get creative and three-dimensional, elaborate on simultaneous events that led to your event or followed it.

Applications: This exercise is useful for checking the logic in a sequence of events. Often in storytelling, we don't show the reader every little thing that happens. The chain-of-events exercise works as a fast outline or timeline that helps you determine how minor actions in your story lead up to a major event, even if those actions aren't shown to the reader. This exercise can also prompt ideas for fiction writing.

9.6 A Sticky Situation

The stickiest situations are the ones without easy answers. Sometimes characters are forced to make decisions when they don't have enough information. If they cut one wire, the entire building will blow up, and everyone dies. Another wire will disarm the bomb. But they don't know which is which.

In other cases, misunderstandings and simple human mistakes lead to uncomfortable (though perhaps not life-threatening) dilemmas. Characters are put in uneasy positions. Friends ask them to lie. They have to choose between the opportunity of a lifetime and their own morals.

These are the scenes that make us squirm but keep us glued to the page. Readers become riveted, because there's no telling what the character will do or how they'll get out of the mess they're in. It's a big what-would-you-do moment, but nobody could possibly know what they would do until they are in that situation themselves.

The Exercise

Come up with three to five sticky situations for your characters. These situations should have no clear or easy answers, but they force a character to make a difficult decision that challenges his or her loyalties or morals. The character may also have to make a decision when he or she doesn't have all the necessary information.

Tips: Here are some examples of sticky situations:

- There's a job opening at the company where Kate works. Her two closest friends apply for the job. After interviewing both of them, Kate's boss asks her to recommend one or the other for the position.

- Jack's two best friends had a falling out a few years ago and no longer speak to each other. Now they're both getting married on the same day, and they both have asked Jack to be the best man.

- A single parent has worked hard to provide for and raise his or her twins, who are fast approaching high-school graduation. Both want to go to college, but there's only enough money to send one to school.

Variations: Instead of coming up with a list of sticky situations, write an entire scene in which your characters find themselves in a sticky situation (feel free to use one of the examples above). If you've ever found yourself in a sticky situation, write about it in a personal essay.

Applications: Sticky situations are great for generating comedy. They create tension and conflict, which are essential elements in writing, especially storytelling.

9.7 If-Then Logic Problems

In a murder mystery, the killer needs a believable motive. In a news story, the facts must be accurate. Everything needs to add up and make sense. Your writing needs to adhere to the rules of logic. If it doesn't, it loses its believability.

Even in nonsensical writing or in speculative fiction, the writer must create a world in which there are rules. If the rules are accidentally broken, readers will notice, and they'll cry foul.

If a character has a broken leg, he can't go dancing. If the driver has a sports car, she couldn't have transported eight people. If the glove doesn't fit, then the suspect couldn't have worn it. Right?

On the other hand, some writers can deftly explain why a character with a broken leg would go dancing, how a driver can fit eight people in a sports car, and why the suspect had an undersized glove.

The Exercise

Below are a series of unlikely scenarios. Each scenario seems impossible. Fix the logic by coming up with plausible explanations.

- A loving mother is convicted of killing her only child. Why was she convicted? Because she confessed. Friends, family, everyone in the community insists she's lying. There's no way she could have done such a thing, but she says she did.

- A young man has everything going for him: a cushy, high-paying job, a beautiful young wife, a child on the way, and a large, lovely home. Things couldn't be better. He's perfectly sane and happy, but for some reason, he gives up everything and runs away.

- There's a girl who can't see anything without her glasses. She's not a candidate for surgery, and her particular condition prevents her from being able to wear contact lenses. She has to wear her glasses at all times; otherwise she can't see. The only time she takes them off is when she's sleeping. Her mother comes into the girl's room and finds her reading a book—without her glasses.

These are the kinds of issues that arise in stories all the time. If you can't come up with a good explanation for the scenarios in your story, you need to find another scenario.

In some cases, these unbelievable situations turn out to be excellent plot twists, and the writer surprises us by explaining how something that seemed impossible actually did happen.

Tips: Whatever you do, don't take the easy way out. The girl who was reading without her glasses was not healed by the magic eye fairy. The young man who ran away from his life did not go insane. Work at finding plausible, reasonable explanations. Make the reader say, "Aha!"

Variations: Instead of coming up with plausible explanations for the scenarios above, develop a few impossible scenarios of your own. See if you can explain them.

Applications: This exercise reminds you that while your readers will suspend disbelief to enjoy your story, you still have a responsibility to make the details as believable as possible. Everything in your writing needs to make sense. Readers love it when strange things happen, as long as a logical explanation follows.

9.8 Solutions

The most effective pieces of writing present a problem and a solution. It doesn't matter if you're writing a story or sales copy. Problem solving is almost always the core element in writing, the hub around which everything else revolves.

In a story, the problem is the protagonist's primary concern, the issue he or she wants to resolve above all else. In a romance, the problem involves relationship issues: the main character is lonely, and she wants to find somebody to love. In a murder mystery, the problem is finding the culprit. Some stories have multiple problems; others focus on a single problem.

In advertising and marketing, good sales copy also focuses on a problem. It compels would-be customers by saying, "You have a problem and our products and services will solve it!" Tired of paying high rates? Want to feel better and look sexier? Need a new car? You've got problems. We've got solutions!

There are two ways to develop problems and solutions in a piece of writing. You can start with the solution, or you can start with the problem. In copywriting, we often start with a solution (a product or service). We have to work backward, figure out how this product or service solves customers' problems, and then explain to the customers how the products or services make their lives better (*you'll save tons of money, look fantastic, and feel great!*).

In fiction writing, we often come up with a problem first, just like in real life. The character is in danger—how does he save himself? The most intriguing problems in fiction seem unsolvable at first. And the cleverest storytellers can get their characters out of the most impossible situations.

Problems and solutions are also integral to nonfiction writing. In nonfiction, all the problems and solutions are provided for you, because everything already happened. However, the writer must explain what happened in a manner that is compelling and builds tension. In her memoir, *Eat, Pray, Love*, Elizabeth Gilbert shares the story of how she was emotionally and spiritually lost. She effectively built a narrative that takes readers on a one-year journey through which she finds herself again. In other words, the nonfiction memoir demonstrates how someone solved a real-life problem; it achieves this through narrative.

The Exercise

Choose one of the following problem-solution exercises:

1. Choose a product on the market (it could be your own book or website) and write a short piece of copy explaining how this product solves a problem. Write a piece that is about 250 words and make it convincing. Focus on the customer's problem and make the solution (your product) enticing.

2. Think of a fictional problem. Put an obstacle in front of your character (maybe the car breaks down in the middle of nowhere while your character is taking a passenger to the hospital for an emergency), and then come up with a believable solution. Write a short scene that presents the problem and the solution.

3. Finally, think of a problem you've experienced or witnessed in real life. Maybe your computer crashed the night before a big essay was due. Perhaps you ran out of toilet paper at a bad time. A problem can be serious or funny, life-threatening or a minor inconvenience. Write a short personal essay (750–1000 words) telling the story of a problem you faced.

Tips: Avoid solving the problems too easily or without a lot of effort on the character's part. If a rich kid runs out of money, a trust fund is not the answer. If a car breaks down, a tow truck should not conveniently drive by right at that moment.

Variations: Instead of choosing one of the problem-solution exercises above, write short pieces about all three, or make a list of problems and solutions that you could use in a writing project.

Applications: If you have your own website, you might use this exercise to write a page pitching your work to the public. If you are working on a novel or a story, use it to create a problem-solution scene in your project.

9.9 Big Themes, Little Scenes

In writing, we often deal with the big things in life: good and evil, faith and science, redemption and sacrifice, birth and death.

Many writers and artists have a specific intent to address big philosophical and ethical issues in their work. Some want to make a statement about culture; others want to explore the question of what it means to be human.

Consider a piece of writing that is concerned with death and the big question: *What happens when we die?* Some people believe there is an afterlife, some believe there is nothing, and some just don't know. In our writing, we might explore the question by showing characters dying and then depicting our own ideas about the afterlife, or we might leave the question open. Instead of answering the question, we encourage readers to think about it and come up with their own answers.

Through the microcosm of a scene in a story or an image in a poem, a writer can grapple with issues and questions that philosophers spend hours, months, and even years contemplating.

The Exercise

Write a short scene dealing with a philosophical theme or issue. Your scene can be fictional, or it can come from real life (your own life, someone else's, or even from a news story or documentary). Start with a basic philosophical question (see exercise 9.1 for some ideas). Then figure out how to turn it into a scene in which the philosophical question is explored through dialogue and action.

Tips: This exercise may require some hard thinking. How do you create a scene in which you take a broad concept and demonstrate it through story? The best thematic material doesn't answer the philosophical questions that it raises (that would be preachy); instead, it makes the audience think and come up with their own answers.

Variations: Instead of writing a full scene, you can write a short outline for a scene, chapter, or story. You can also integrate this exercise into a project you are working on.

Applications: In storytelling, real or fictional, big themes tend to resonate well, especially with smart audiences who appreciate art that makes them think, question, and see the world in new ways. Thought-provoking literature is far more celebrated than literature that is preachy or dogmatic.

9.10 Politics and Religion

Today, politics and religion are so commercialized, sometimes it's difficult to sift through all the talking points and identify the core philosophical ideals upon which political and religious beliefs are based. Politics and religion concern themselves with some very, very big questions: Who should get what? What rights do we, as a people, have? How do we remove threats from our society, and what constitutes a threat? When do we help other people? How? What's fair?

You will inevitably run up against these issues in your writing. Even if you have no intention of bringing your political and religious beliefs into your work, it will probably happen eventually.

What happens when you're writing about someone whose religious or political beliefs differ from your own? Are you only going to write about people who are like you? Are all of your characters going to think exactly the same way you do?

That could get pretty boring. And it's not realistic. We're living in an increasingly diverse and interconnected world. It's getting harder and harder for people to cordon themselves off from other cultures and ideologies.

The Exercise

Invent a character who is your opposite in terms of spiritual beliefs and political convictions. However, (here's the catch), the character cannot be a villain. Write a scene in which the character demonstrates his or her beliefs through action.

Tips: Some writers struggle with the concept of making characters (especially "good" characters) behave in ways that the writer thinks are immoral. Vegetarians may not want to work with characters who hunt, eat meat, or work as butchers. If the story calls for a butcher, the worst thing a vegetarian can do is create a special storyline in which that butcher has some experience that causes him to become a vegetarian. He's a butcher! Leave him that way (unless the story's main theme is conversion to vegetarianism). Don't use this exercise or concept as a tool for preaching through fiction. Focus on telling a good story. The best fiction doesn't make moral commentary every step of the way.

Variations: Instead of developing a fictional character, write about a real person. Find someone whose beliefs are completely opposite your own. Create a list of philosophical questions about religion and politics, and conduct an interview with this person. Go for deep, probing questions, and do not load them with your own feelings or thoughts. Do not challenge the person you're interviewing or engage in debate or argument. Your job is to ask questions and record the answers. When the interview is complete, write a summary about what you learned.

Applications: As a fiction writer, you have to be able to put yourself in other people's shoes. Mystery writers aren't killers, but they have to write characters who are. You can model all your characters after yourself, but they will come across as generic. Push yourself to explore people who are different from you.

Chapter 10: Article Writing and Blogging

Addressing an audience and building a platform

10.1 Titles and Headlines

A title or headline is the first point of contact that a reader will have with your writing. It's your introduction, a chance to entice and intrigue readers so they want to buy your book or read your article. An effective title piques a reader's curiosity and provides some idea of what the piece is about.

Some authors use titles as part of their brand. Sue Grafton is working her way through the alphabet with her Kinsey Millhone series (*A is for Alibi, B is for Burglar*, etc.). Many romance novelists use words like *kiss, love,* or *dance* in their titles. In the sci-fi realm, anything associated with space is fair game: *galaxy, universe, Mars*, and *stars*. And a well placed mythological term, such as *dragon* or *wizard*, clearly marks a fantasy novel.

In addition to book titles, many authors have a separate title for a series. This allows the author to use two different titles on a single piece of work. New readers will be drawn in by the book title, and existing fans will gravitate toward the series title.

In poetry, titles can be more abstract. A poem's title may seem irrelevant to the poem. Many poets take a word or phrase from the poem and use it as a title. Others will use a title that functions as part of the poem. The best poem titles evoke an image and give the reader an indication of what the poem will feel like.

Magazines use headlines prominently displayed on the front cover to entice customers. Newspapers use them to draw readers into a story, and bloggers, as many of you know, use headlines to generate buzz, links, and tweets.

The Exercise

Choose one of your writing projects or ideas and make a list of possible titles. Don't run off a quick list. Take some time to contemplate each title. Consider how it will resonate with readers and the impact it will have your project's success. Make sure the titles and headlines you write represent the piece accurately. Avoid words and phrases that are misleading.

Tips: Look to some successful works by authors you admire to get ideas for titles. Peruse magazines, newspapers, and blogs for headline ideas.

Variations: If you don't have any writing projects that need titles, then make a list of titles from some of your favorite books, magazines, movies, TV shows, articles, and poems. Develop alternative titles for these pieces.

Applications: Every piece of writing has to be titled, and a title or headline is essential in selling the piece to its audience. Developing catchy, intriguing titles is an essential writing skill.

10.2 How-to Articles

In the old days, if you wanted to learn how to do something, you had to go through a lot of effort. You went to the library and checked out a book. You became an apprentice or took an entry-level job so you could learn the basics. You took classes. You started from scratch.

These days, instructions for everything imaginable are available on the Internet, and most of them are free. You can learn how to ride a bike, build a house, and start a business with a few quick clicks.

It's pretty cool that we now have free and open access to so much knowledge. What's even cooler is that someone has to write all those how-to articles.

How-to pieces and step-by-step instruction guides are among the most popular articles found in magazines and on the web. Readers gravitate toward these types of articles, because there's a promise that they will learn something new and obtain something they want: "How to Get a Rockin' Body," "How to Save Thousands of Dollars with Tax Write-Offs," "How to Find the Love of Your Life."

People are on a perpetual quest for sex, love, health, money, and good looks. How-to articles promise to show them the path to fulfilling their desires.

Tutorials, on the other hand, show readers how to do a specific task. These step-by-step instructional articles take the reader through a process: "How to Change a Furnace Filter," "How to Self-Publish a Novel," "How to Organize Your Closet."

The Exercise

Write a how-to article or step-by-step tutorial. Start by picking something you know how to do. You can write a general how-to article or a detailed step-by-step piece. Choose something you know a lot about, and write a clear, polished piece.

Tips: We tend to assume all the things we know how to do are common knowledge. Yet there are things you know how to do that your coworkers, friends, and family don't know how to do.

If you have a blog or website, then write something that relates to your site's topic so you can publish it when it's done.

Variations: Write a list of potential how-to articles about things you know how to do, then go online and search for publications that might accept your article as a submission.

Applications: How-to articles are popular in magazines and on blogs. If you have a fresh idea that will entice readers, you might be able to get it published (you might even get paid for it). You can also use your how-to article on your own blog or as a guest blog post.

10.3 List Articles

List articles are just as popular as how-to articles. They are appealing because they tend to be clear and well organized. Expectations are set as soon as the reader sees the title. For example, in a book titled *101 Creative Writing Exercises*, you expect that inside that book, you'll find 101 creative writing exercises. You know what you're going to get, and you know how much of it you're going to get. These articles and books seem like a smart investment, so readers embrace them.

Lists can be instructional in nature. You might write a list article on "Ten Ways to Improve Your Writing." They can also be inspirational: "Twelve Habits of Happy People." Lists can be trivial: "The Twenty Best Movies of the Twentieth Century." They can be promotional: "The Fifteen Best Websites for Storytellers."

There are plenty of opportunities for writing list articles about any subjects that interest you.

The Exercise

Write a list article. Choose a topic that you're passionate about or that you are knowledgeable about.

Tips: Start your article with an introduction. It should be one to three paragraphs. Format your list using numbers or bullets. Write one sentence or a short paragraph for each list item explaining why its inclusion on the list is warranted. Conclude your article with a one-paragraph summary.

Variations: You can combine a how-to article and a list article: "Ten Steps to Writing a Novel." These articles include lists but are also instructional in nature.

Applications: List articles are extremely popular in magazines and on blogs. If you write a good piece, you can probably get it published.

10.4 Everyone's a Critic (Book Review)

We've all read books we've loved, seen movies we hated, and then spread the word: *You've got to see this show! Wait till it's out on DVD. You want to know? Buy the book.*

There's a big difference between saying something is good or bad and explaining why it's good or bad. There are reasons you love one book and can't get past the first chapter in another. Maybe you didn't like one story because the writing was too obscure, or the characters had no personality. In another story, the plot is packed with puzzles, and the characters feel like friends. What keeps you interested in a piece of writing, and what turns you off?

A well-written review is thoughtful. It looks for the good and the bad and does more than spout the author's opinion. It analyzes the work and determines what's working and what's not working.

Writing book reviews forces you to evaluate a work carefully. Too often, we close a book or walk away from a movie with our thumbs up or down without trying to understand why.

The Exercise

Choose a book you've read and write a detailed review of it. Your piece should start with what you liked about the book and should also list areas where the work was flawed. Address the piece to potential readers.

Tips: Do not write a synopsis or retell the story; your job is to explain to the audience why they should (or shouldn't) read the book, without including spoilers. Finally, if you didn't like the book, add a statement about who might like it. If you loved it, add a comment about what type of audience might not enjoy or appreciate it.

Variations: You can also do this exercise for a movie, play, or TV show.

Applications: If you become a published author, your work will inevitably get critiqued and reviewed. Being on the other side of a review is good practice. Also, by critiquing and reviewing other artists' work, you'll see your own work from a fresh perspective. Many writers make a living (or some income) writing reviews. And many readers (and writers) post reviews on the web to help others make better decisions about what to read and watch.

10.5 Critiques

Critiques are similar to reviews except they are for writers rather than potential readers; a critique explains what's working and not working to the author in an effort to help a fellow writer improve his or her work.

In a critique, you start by listing the strengths of the piece. Then, you list the areas that could be improved. Don't try to change the piece into what you would have done as a writer; take it for what it is.

Finally, a proper critique discusses the work, not the person who created it. Your objective is to use positive, supportive language framed in the context of how the piece could be improved.

The Exercise

Choose a piece of writing and compose a critique. You can use a book, short story, poem, article, or blog post. You will address the critique to the author, but you will not send it to the author. Also, your critique will discuss the work, not the person who created it.

The length of your critique will depend on how long the piece of writing is and how deeply you evaluate it.

Tips: You should also look for spelling, grammar, and punctuation mistakes, as well as typographical errors.

Variations: You can also do this exercise using a movie, a TV show, or any kind of story or art medium.

Applications: This exercise teaches you to look at a piece of writing objectively and assess it thoughtfully in an effort to consider how it might be improved. Writing critiques will help you build skills that will benefit your own writing projects.

10.6 The Weekly Column

There was a time when a writer could dream about landing a weekly column with a newspaper. If you got a spot at a big paper, money was good. You could make a living writing one column per week.

These days, weekly columns are on the endangered species list. More and more magazines and newspapers are going digital. Some of them easily find writers who are willing to work for free. As we all know, working for free might be good experience, and it never hurts to get a byline, but it sure doesn't put food on the table.

Highly skilled writers tend to demand some kind of compensation for their work, so the quality of columns has suffered considerably. There are still good ones out there, but we have to look harder to find them.

Blogs swept in and gave writers their own publishing platforms. However, blogs don't come with a readership (or a paycheck). If you want to make money or build an audience with your blog, you have to do more than write a post every week. You have to promote and market your site. It's a lot of work, but many writers find that there's a nice payoff, eventually.

There are many types of blogs. For the purpose of this exercise, we'll look at blogs that are similar to newspaper columns. Here's how it works: Every week, the writer shares a story along with his or her thoughts or opinions about it. In some cases, columns are personal. The show

Sex and the City featured a columnist who wrote weekly pieces about her romantic escapades in New York City. Each week, she shared her personal story and waxed philosophical on love, romance, and friendship. Other topical columns might address politics, religion, food, or entertainment. Columns are written from a personal perspective; over time, the audience comes to know the columnist.

The Exercise

Start by choosing a theme or topic for your column, and then, write your first column. Make sure you tell a story, address an issue, and weave your personal thoughts and experiences through the piece.

Tips: Columns are a bit like reflective journaling or personal essays in that they're very much about the columnist's own ideas, attitudes, and experiences regarding the subject matter. They are written in first person.

Variations: Instead of writing a column, write a proposal for a column. Include the focal subject matter, explain why you're qualified to write about this issue, and list some personal experiences you've had related to the topic. Make sure you identify an audience for your column.

Applications: This is a great exercise if you're thinking about launching a blog (or if you already have one). Many of today's bloggers write column-style posts. While columnist jobs are on the decline, they are still out there; there's also a good chance that as the web matures, this style of writing (and paid gigs) will become more commonplace.

10.7 *Wanna Be a Blogger?*

Blogs are here, and they're here to stay. In early 2012, Blogpulse identified over 182,397,015 blogs on the web with over eighty thousand new blogs launching every day.

If you're planning on being a writer, either professionally or as a hobby, then you are living in the right era. Blogs have freed writers in numerous ways. They provide a relatively easy-to-use platform for self-publishing and building a readership. They also make it easy to find, connect, and network with other writers.

The blogging community is enormous. In fact, it's more like a universe. In the greater blog universe, there are tons of galaxies—groups of blogs that revolve around specific topics and ideas. There are hobby blogs, fan blogs, professional blogs, news and information blogs. You can find blogs about movies, TV shows, careers, art, philosophy, science, pets, sports, and literature—if people are interested in it, then there's a blog about it.

Some blogs don't have a topic at all; bloggers simply write and publish their personal journals.

While many technophiles have leveraged blogging as a route to professional success, few professionals have benefitted from blogs as much as writers. Fifty years ago, a writer had to rely on literary agents, professional marketers, PR firms, publishing houses, and bookstores. Today, with a little enterprise, a writer can use a blog to connect with other writers, build a readership, and promote and sell their work.

The Exercise

Write a short business plan for your author's blog. Begin by choosing the niche or subject you'll write about. Include the following details:

- Write a short description of your blog (try to keep it to fewer than one hundred words).

- State the blog's purpose or mission.

- Identify the audience for your blog.

- Make a list of ten titles for future blog posts.

- Give your blog a name.

- Write a paragraph explaining why you're qualified to write on this subject.

Tips: If you're unfamiliar with blogs, then do a little research before tackling this exercise. Peruse at least ten blogs. Try to explore a mix of topics. Look for a few different author blogs, a few blogs about writing, and a few that are not writing-related. Think about your other hobbies and interests, and then look for blogs in those niches.

Variations: If you already have a blog, use this exercise as an opportunity to improve it. Make sure your blog has an "About" page or a "Bio." Identify your blog's core purpose and readership. Create an editorial calendar or stockpile a few extra posts.

Applications: If you plan on being a professional writer, you will most definitely need a blog. Start planning now!

10.8 The Op-Ed

In traditional journalism, an editorial is an opinion piece written by a magazine or newspaper's editor or some other member of the editorial staff. An op-ed (which is an abbreviation of *opposite the editorial page*) is an opinion piece by a named writer who is not a staff member.

Some op-eds are written by regular contributors. These are writers who have established a relationship with the publication. Others are written by well-known experts or professionals in a particular field, which is usually related to the subject of the piece. The op-ed provides a platform where people (ordinary people, experts, or celebrities) can share their opinions on a given subject or issue.

An op-ed can function as a career booster. Politicians, for example, often write op-eds. This gives them a platform to state their positions on various issues and an opportunity to win voters. It's also a platform where people can review or critique art, events, and cultural movements. Some publications publish op-eds in which a writer responds to an article or editorial that appeared in an earlier issue.

Op-eds can deal with world issues and controversies, or they can deal with subjects of a more personal nature. For example, op-eds often remark on the state of the nation, wars, politics, scandals, and high-profile court cases. However, they can also examine issues surrounding child rearing, healthy (or unhealthy) living, and a host of other community and personal issues.

The Exercise

Write an op-ed about an issue or problem that concerns you. Before you begin, identify a target publication and audience.

Tips: In an op-ed, you'll make a personal argument for or against something that is of current interest to the readership of the target publication.

Variations: Read three to five op-ed pieces. Note your observations about the writers' voices, tones, and positions, as well as the arguments they use to back up their claims. Are the pieces emotional, rational, or a balance of both?

Applications: One way to start getting published is to write and submit op-eds to your local paper. You can also write letters to the editor.

10.9 You're the Expert

You know a little bit about a lot of things, but there are a few things you know a lot about. And knowledge is power.

One of the traditional duties of a writer is to collect and redistribute knowledge and information. After all, writers are responsible for textbooks, instruction manuals, and reference collections, like encyclopedias.

The Internet has made this type of material more accessible than ever before. People no longer have to trudge down to the library or buy expensive sets of encyclopedias, which quickly become outdated, to research and learn. They just log in and look it up.

The Exercise

Choose something you know a lot about. In fact, choose the one thing you know the most about. It could be a subject you studied in school. It could be a video game you've played for countless hours. It could be something simple, like the parts of speech in the English language, or it could be something complicated, like how photosynthesis works. Write an informational article explaining this thing to a layperson—someone with zero experience or knowledge about the topic.

Tips: Assume your reader is ignorant about the subject. If you're doing a piece on photosynthesis, assume your reader doesn't know what carbon dioxide is. If you're doing a complex piece, break it down into simple steps and definitions.

Variations: If you'd rather not get into the nitty-gritty about your subject matter, write a statement explaining your own expertise. Why are you qualified to write about photosynthesis?

Applications: Many writers have built careers around writing about what they know best or what they can research and explain to readers.

10.10 Conducting Research

All good writers know the value and importance of conducting proper research. Research is necessary in every form and genre of writing, so it's essential for all writers to learn how to conduct credible research.

Even journal writers and memoirists find that they have to conduct research occasionally. Let's say you're writing in your journal about a concert you attended, but you can't remember the name of the opening band. You'll have to do a little research to find out who it was. In a memoir, research might involve conducting interviews with people who can help you remember the details of your own past.

Poets may need to research their subject matter, especially when they're writing a highly focused poem. If you're doing a sonnet on tigers, you might read up on the species so you have plenty of material to work with.

The Exercise

Pick a subject that you know a bit about but in which you are not thoroughly knowledgeable. Spend an hour or two conducting research about your subject, and then write a short piece about it. You can write a story, poem, or article.

Tips: If you decide to write a nonfiction piece, make sure you cite the sources from which you gathered information. You don't have to spend weeks poring over books and journals, but try to learn a few facts that you can use. Take notes and make sure you write down the names (titles and authors) of the works you referenced.

Variations: You can also apply this exercise to one of your current writing projects. If you're working on a novel in which one of your characters is an astronaut, and you know nothing about astronauts, you can interview one, watch a documentary about astronauts and space travel, or read a book or article on the lifestyle of astronauts. Then write a character sketch based on your research.

Applications: Research is integral to good writing. Readers have sharp eyes and will catch you if the facts aren't correct. As a writer, you should always be aware of what you know and what you don't know. You should also learn how to gather the information you need for any given project.

Chapter 11: Creativity

Gathering ideas and looking for inspiration

11.1 Maps and Legends

In fiction, setting is one of the four key elements (along with character, plot, and theme). It is essential for readers to have a sense of place, and in order for that to happen, the writer must have a deep understanding of a story's setting.

In a complex piece of writing that covers a lot of geographic ground, maps can help a writer maintain a story's geography. With modern technology, rendering a map for a piece of writing is easier than ever.

Exploring maps and making your own maps are excellent exercises in creative thinking. Maps exist for a wide variety of physical places: worlds, nations, neighborhoods, underground tunnel systems, weather systems, and the stars. Maps show you new ways to look at the world of your writing, allowing you to imagine how place might influence events.

What if you're writing about a place that doesn't exist? The answer is simple: you make your own map.

The Exercise

Choose a piece of writing that you're working on, and render a map that shows where events unfold. You might need a map of the world, or you may need a simple blueprint of a house. You can search for maps online, print them out, and then add symbols (dots, stars, and lines) representing significant locations and movements from your piece of writing. Make sure you include a legend that explains the symbols and what they mean. If you have made up your own place for a story, then create a map from scratch.

Tips: You can print a map, trace it, and then fill it with various elements from your story. Be creative. Use color coding for different characters. Use symbols for the most significant events. Use lines to show travel routes. Remember, a map is merely a drawn representation of a place. You can map anything from a room or a garden to an ocean or a galaxy.

Variations: If you don't have an adequate piece of writing to use for this exercise, then map a story from a favorite book.

Applications: Some books include maps to help readers visualize setting. Articles and essays often include maps. This exercise encourages you to think in spatial terms, and it inspires deeper creativity in your writing by engaging in a nonwriting activity that informs your written work.

11.2 The Name Game

What's in a name? That which we call a rose

By any other name would smell as sweet;

—from *Romeo and Juliet* by William Shakespeare

This famous quote from Shakespeare suggests that a name is meaningless, that meaning exists only in the thing the name represents. The word *rose* is unimportant. The scent of the rose is what matters.

Names are words used to represent people, places, and things. They are words. And words, by definition, have meaning.

What if Luke Skywalker's name had been Joe Smith? Would we fall in love with a wizard named Harry Johnson instead of Harry Potter? Does Suellen O'Hara's name have the same resonance as her sister's (Scarlett O'Hara)? How would we feel about an adventuring archeologist named Lenny Jones rather than Indiana Jones?

And names are not limited to characters. What if Neverland was just some crazy island without a name? What if New York was called Aberdine? What if a computer was called a robrain? What if our planet was called Dearth?

Names matter.

The Exercise

Take a break from your writing projects and create a repository of names. For this exercise, come up with a minimum of twenty-five names. You can name characters, places, gadgets and devices, companies, planets, species, and anything else that you can think of.

Tips: Start a name file or name notebook where you can jot down your ideas for names along with a few notes. Use baby-name dictionaries to look up the meanings of names, and use names that lend deeper meaning to your writing. You can also search online for name generators, which are especially useful in the science fiction and fantasy genres.

Variations: Write a list of your twenty-five favorite names from literature and pop culture. Try to come up with a mix of names, real and imagined. Include names for people, places, and things.

Applications: In your creative work, you will undoubtedly need to name various entities. This is good practice.

11.3 The Taste Test

Food. It is essential for survival. We need it for nourishment, but we've also come to enjoy our food. We appreciate its taste and celebrate chefs who prepare delightful dishes. Food is art that melts on the tongue.

As writers, we appreciate that food is uniquely capable of triggering all five senses simultaneously. We smell chocolate chip cookies baking in the oven. We savor the rich, sweet taste as they crumble and melt in our mouths. Then we gulp a cold splash of milk to wash it all down.

Food can function as many things in a piece of writing. It can be the object of a quest in a story where characters are trying to survive. It can provide sensory cues in a poem about a grandmother's kitchen. Food can be a metaphor or a symbol, or it can be the subject matter in pieces of nonfiction: restaurant reviews, recipes, cookbooks, and cooking-show scripts.

The Exercise

For this exercise, you will dine and write about it in succulent detail. Your task is to set out in search of food. Hot and spicy, sweet and sour, rich, light, healthy, or artery clogging, sit down and enjoy a delightful meal.

Make your own meal or visit your favorite restaurant. After your dining experience, figure out a way to work the meal into a piece of writing. You can create a scene in which your characters enjoy a similar meal, or you can write a personal essay about your dining experience.

Tips: Take notes while you're eating. Use all five senses to describe your experience.

Variations: Make a list of words and phrases to describe your dining experience. Write out your favorite recipe, or write a review of your favorite restaurant or food product.

Applications: Food writing finds its way into every form and genre. If you are a foodie—or just someone who appreciates good old-fashioned home cooking—you'll find that writing about food makes your work more visceral. If you've ever read about food and found that it made your mouth water, you have experienced this firsthand. And if you're really into it, you can always become a food writer.

More importantly, this exercise shows you how to experience life first and write about it later.

11.4 It's Your Holiday

Most of us take holidays for granted. Some holidays have been reduced to massive spending, reckless gifting, and obnoxious amounts of eating. Others are a day off, time to catch up on errands, clean the house, or spend a day luxuriating at the beach.

Holidays are steeped in meaning. Each one is based on something deemed important enough to warrant a day of recognition and celebration. While holidays vary across cultures, they are present everywhere and throughout history.

A holiday starts out as a significant event, one that has an impact on a culture's history. Some holidays celebrate the life, birth, or death of groups or individuals who have changed the world for the better. Customs that reflect the meaning of a holiday evolve: decorations, food, attire, rituals, and art come together to mark the day.

Considering all the great people who have lived and died and all the significant events that have shaped our world, it's actually surprising that we have so few holidays.

The Exercise

Create a brand new holiday. Start with something or someone you believe warrants annual recognition on a national or global scale. You can also build holidays around natural events like solstices and equinoxes.

Tips: Before you start this exercise, choose one holiday and do a little research to learn about its origin and how it has evolved.

Consider the following as you develop your holiday:

- What does this holiday celebrate or honor?
- When is the holiday, and how long does it last?
- How do people gather? In public spaces? In homes?
- Do people dress formally or casually? In costume?
- What foods are traditionally served? Do people fast?
- What rituals are observed?

- How is art incorporated? Music, dance, stories, poems, and performances are integral to most holidays.

Variations: Change one of the holidays we already celebrate. Can you improve upon it? Can you bring it back to its roots or make it more meaningful?

Applications: Writers benefit from having a broad understanding of culture, and holidays are a key component of any culture. Holidays have inspired poetry, songs, and stories. If you write speculative fiction, you might even find a home for your newly invented holiday.

11.5 What's Your Superpower?

What if you could fly or make yourself invisible? What if you could heal with a touch or read minds? Superpowers like these are the stuff of science fiction.

Savants and prodigies are superheroes in their own rights, and they exist in the real world.

A prodigy is someone (often a young child) with an extraordinary talent or ability: a twelve-year-old college graduate or a fifteen-year-old Nobel Prize contender.

A savant is someone who is an expert, whereas someone with savant syndrome (savantism) is a person with a developmental disability who also has superhuman expertise, ability, or brilliance in a particular area.

The Exercise

Create a new superpower. Write a clear description of it, and make sure you include the following:

- Explain how the superpower is obtained.

- Invent a weakness (like Superman's kryptonite) that can counteract that superpower.
- Describe how someone might use this superpower for good or evil.

If you're so inclined, create a character who possesses this power and write a story about it.

Tips: Stay away from overdone powers like flight, invisibility, and super strength. Avoid psychic powers like telepathy and telekinesis. Think up something fresh: for example, someone who can breathe in outer space.

Variations: If science fiction isn't your thing or if you're tired of superheroes, then come up with a character who is a prodigy or who has savantism.

Applications: Many stories, both real and fictional, feature ordinary people in extraordinary circumstances. In this exercise, you flip convention on its head and create a character who is extraordinary. How does an extraordinary person fit into the ordinary world?

11.6 Observation Station

You might think that your creative ideas spontaneously erupt from your mind. In a sense, that's true, but these ideas also manifest from all of the observations you've made and experiences you've had.

Every moment is an opportunity to bear witness. Each experience you have is a chance to examine the human condition. Every second of life is a seed from which creative ideas can grow.

As creative people, it's essential for us to understand inspiration and to avoid blaming pseudoconditions like writer's block when we don't feel like doing our work. Writer's block is easily cured once you understand how to cultivate ideas from everyday life.

The Exercise

This exercise asks you to put your writing aside and explore the world in search of inspiration. Your task is to get up and get out, visit a public space, and note your observations. Monitor the people at a mall. Could they become characters in your story? Examine the environment in a national park. Could it become the subject of your next poem? When you've finished recording your observations, return to your writing space and look for ways you can use your observations in your writing.

Tips: Be on the lookout for the unusual: someone wearing odd clothing, a misshapen tree, and unique buildings. Engage all of your senses. Make it a point to note the sights, sounds, smells, and textures. If edibles are present, make notes about the tastes. Use vivid, sensuous language to describe your observations in your notebook.

Variations: If you can't get out of the house or the office, then try to take a new angle on your own familiar habitats. What would your home or workplace look like to an outside observer? Write a descriptive essay about it.

Applications: The better we understand the creative process and the steps involved in generating ideas, the better we can maintain our creativity and cultivate creative thinking.

11.7 The Story of Music

We writers often look to the obvious for inspiration. We pore over news articles and reflect on our own experiences. We ponder our favorite stories and think about how they can inform our work. We can also look to other art forms to inspire and guide our creativity.

Song lyrics often tell a story. What about the music itself? The crescendo of a string section fills a listener with tension. The loud boom of a base drum evokes a sense of impending doom, while the sharp tap of a snare renders a sense of purpose.

Each movement, instrument, melody, and rhythm has the potential to take you deep inside your own imagination where stories are waiting to be discovered.

The Exercise

Listen to a piece of instrumental music. Try to find or use a piece that resonates with you, a piece you love. Sit or lie still as you listen to it once, letting yourself become one with the music. Then listen to it a second time, and as you listen, write down the images that fill your head. Can you turn these into stories or poems? Think about how this music and the way it affects you can be used to inspire your next writing project.

Tips: For your first listen, turn the lights low, and sit back or lie down in a comfortable position. Use headphones for an optimal auditory experience. If you can't use headphones, set the volume comfortably loud. Get lost in the music. The second time you listen, as you write down your notes, feel free to use doodles and drawings to render what the music inspired you to imagine. Some musical genres you might explore include classical, world, and jazz, as well as movie soundtracks and TV scores.

Variations: You can, of course, cull inspiration from lyrical pieces of music. Choose a song with lyrics and let the words and music inspire writing ideas, or spend some time creating playlists that you can listen to during your writing sessions.

Applications: Learning how the arts inform one another is extremely helpful in creative work. This exercise shows you how to look beyond the obvious for sources of inspiration.

11.8 Angles

There is a parable, which originated in India and has crossed over to many other cultures, about six blind men and an elephant, which originated in India and has crossed over to many other cultures.

The short story is that six blind men are asked to explain what an elephant looks like. Each man touches one part of the elephant, and then they all offer different descriptions of the same animal. They are all correct, although their descriptions vary. However, they are also incorrect, since their limited experiences of the elephant only allowed each of them to describe one small part of the greater whole.

This story has been used to illustrate a range of truths and fallacies in philosophy. For our purposes, it serves to remind us that our perception of the world is highly dependent upon our particular perspective.

The Exercise

Write a description of something, looking at it from a new angle. You will write a clear, concise description from an unfamiliar perspective.

Tips: Below are some ideas to help you get started:

- You usually view your home from the inside or from your backyard or driveway. Go outside and view your house from a new angle. What do you see?

- In your daily activities, you follow many of the same routes to work, stores, and restaurants. Take a different route. How does it change the experience?

- Look around at the many objects that surround you. We generally view dishes, cups, and bowls right side up. We look at things from the front. Choose an object and turn it around or upside down. What do you see?

- What if you were from another country? What if you spoke another language? How does your culture look to someone from the outside? How would our world look to an alien?

Variations: As an alternative, pretend you are either an alien from a faraway planet or a member of a tribe that is technologically primitive. Choose an object, gadget, or device, and come up with ideas for what it might be used for. Here's an example: a tribesman finds a glass soda bottle, blows into it, and determines that it is a musical instrument.

Applications: Creativity is at its peak when you are looking at the world from a fresh perspective. You can find new ways of looking at ordinary things by simply moving to a new position or regarding an object as an unknown entity.

11.9 A World of Color

The best writing is full of life and color. Although text is usually printed or displayed in black and white, we have to make our writing descriptive enough to fill readers' heads with vivid, colorful images.

Working with color is a great way to promote creative thinking. Normally, writers work with words and concepts. Stepping away from our grayscale documents and into a world of color triggers creative ideas and serves as a reminder to infuse our work with imagery.

With print technology becoming cheaper, and with the many options available on word processing software, it's easier than ever for writers to literally bring color to their words. But making text purple or green often backfires. It tells readers that the writing is not colorful enough and needs some design help. In fact, colored text often comes across as gimmicky. Try to avoid it.

The Exercise

For this exercise, you will put all your writing aside and work strictly with color. You can use crayons, markers, or paints. You can cut out pieces of colored paper. Do not try to render a scene or specific image. Instead, use chunks of color in abstract shapes to create a color composition.

Tips: Vary your colors and shapes. Try mixing and layering your colors. Use simple but varied shapes: squares, circles, ovals, triangles, and odd or unusual abstract shapes.

Variations: If you have a hard time working in the abstract, feel free to use basic images as a basis for your composition: trees, houses, stars, boxes, etc. Try to create a scene.

Applications: Creativity sometimes needs to come from outside our craft. Writers can get so caught up in words that our ideas becomes stale or stagnant. This exercise forces us out of the world of black-and-white words and into a more colorful universe.

11.10 The Incubator

Many creative professionals and hobbyists have found that creative ideas need time to incubate. In other words, you don't start working on an idea as soon as it occurs to you. You mull it over, give it some time to take root, and wait for it to mature a little before you start executing it.

Some of us are full of ideas, and some of us spend a lot of time waiting or searching for ideas. In either case, the trick is to figure out which ideas are worth pursuing. Sometimes, an idea that seems brilliant at first turns out to be a big flop, whereas a mediocre idea evolves into a masterpiece.

How do you know which ideas are worth your time and energy? Let them marinate for a while. Experiment with the ones that seem most interesting. The ideas and concepts that haunt you are the ones to pursue. Those are the ones you should commit to.

The Exercise

For this exercise, you will create an incubator for your creative ideas. This is a special place where you store ideas and items that inspire you. Once you've created your incubator, you should rifle through it every week or every month, so your ideas stay fresh in your head. When you feel an idea is ready for production, pull it out and start developing it.

Your incubator can be a box, a jar, a folder on your computer, or a special notebook.

To get started, go through your notes and journals and try to find five to ten ideas you've had but never developed. These will be the first ideas you put in your incubator.

Tips: You may find that you need to organize your ideas. For a single novel idea, you might have several related ideas: characters, plots, and scenes. You might want to keep your poetry ideas separate from your fiction ideas. You can organize your incubator in any way that's comfortable for you. If you're using a box, you might want to use file folders or envelopes to organize things. If you're using a jar or basket, you might use colored papers for different projects or categories. In a special notebook, you can use page markers or divide the notebook into sections. In a computer folder, you can organize ideas with subfolders. Your incubator can hold notes, photos, and other images—anything that is related to your idea.

Variations: As you surf the web, you might come across items of interest or sites that contain information or images that you want to use for inspiration. Create a special bookmarks folder for these items.

Applications: Nothing's worse than losing a good idea. Make sure you put your ideas in the incubator as soon as they occur to you. That might mean wrenching yourself out of bed or pausing in the middle of dinner to jot down a note. But once you start storing your ideas and reviewing them regularly, you'll find that more and more ideas keep coming. Pretty soon, you'll have plenty of fodder for writing.

Chapter 12: Moving Forward with Your Writing

As your adventures in writing continue, there will be times when the sentences come effortlessly and times when you strain to squeeze out a word or two. You'll get frustrated as you work through draft after draft in an effort to polish your work for a reading audience.

If you submit your work to agents or editors, you can count on getting plenty of rejections before seeing your name in print. If you self-publish, you'll struggle to find your first readers, and you'll have to become an entrepreneur, managing everything from the editing to the cover art.

Writing requires a tremendous amount of patience and dedication. Just as athletes train and performers rehearse, writers must practice their craft. Each rejection slip brings you one step closer to getting published. And every crumpled-up draft that gets tossed in the recycle bin is a step toward reaching your full potential as a writer.

The writers who succeed are not the ones with the most talent or best mastery of the craft. They are the ones who refuse to give up.

Here are a few final tips to help you as you move forward with your creative writing:

1. Read. Curl up with a good novel, brush up on your nonfiction reading, flip through some poetry collections. Reading is the single best way to naturally acquire writing skills and inspiration. Read as much and as often as you can, and your writing will improve dramatically.

2. Write. In order to be a writer, you must write. Try to write every single day. Some days, you'll write several pages. Other days, you might squeeze out a paragraph. But you're writing, and that's all that matters. Even if you can only dedicate a few minutes to writing each day, it will become an ingrained habit.

3. Revise: proofread, edit, and polish. It's blatantly obvious when a piece of writing has not been properly polished. Typos, grammatical mistakes, and poorly written sentences will offend anyone who attempts to read your work. In other words, you'll turn readers off. Put your best work forward.

4. Brush up on grammar. It's rare for a piece of writing to be so amazing that readers are willing to ignore bad grammar. Many writers are lazy in this area, because learning grammar is a lot of work, and it's academic work rather than creative work. The good news is that once you learn the rules, they will be with you forever. Pick up a stylebook or grammar guide, and take time to look up anything you don't know.

5. Develop your skills. You will learn that some aspects of writing come easily to you (maybe you're great at dialogue), but other aspects are a challenge (your plots are full of holes). Once you accept your weaknesses, you can work on eliminating them through practice and study.

6. Find your process. Your process is the series of steps you take to complete a project. Experiment with different techniques and strategies from discovery writing to outlining, and find what works best for you.

7. Share your work and invite feedback. One of the quickest ways to improve your writing is through feedback. Get a well-read person to review your work and give it a critique. Embrace the feedback, even if it hurts, and then put it to work for you by ironing out all the wrinkles that your friendly reader found.

8. Collect tools and resources. Writers don't need much. For centuries, a pen and paper were the only tools required. Nowadays, we have computers, programs and apps, and a host of resources from books to blogs that help us become more productive, professional, and skilled.

9. Cultivate creativity. Have fun with your writing. Fill it with color or scale it back to a minimalist style. Try new words and off-the-wall images. Take breaks from writing to experiment with other art forms. Do creativity exercises. This will keep your creative juices flowing and help you see your own creative problems from new angles, so you can solve them and produce the best work possible.

9. Engage with the writing community. These days, there is no excuse for failing to connect with other writers. There are plenty of blogs, forums, and social networking sites that make it easy for writers to connect and forge relationships. Be supportive of other writers, and they will support you in return.

Make a conscious commitment to strive for better writing every day. And most importantly, keep writing.

More Adventures in Writing

1200 Creative Writing Prompts is designed to do one thing: inspire you.

- 500 fiction prompts cover a range of genres: literary, suspense, thriller, mystery, science fiction, fantasy, horror, romance, historical, humor, satire, children's, and young adult.
- 400 poetry prompts inspire you with subjects, images, and word lists.
- 300 creative nonfiction prompts motivate you to write memoirs, personal essays, journal entries, and encourage you to explore your writing goals and habits.

Available from your favorite online booksellers. Learn more at http://www.writingforward.com/books.

Improve Your Writing

10 Core Practices for Better Writing presents ten lifelong practices that any writer can adopt. Each practice improves and strengthens your writing over the long term, leading to high-caliber work.

- Explore beneficial practices that bring out the excellence in your writing.
- Discover tools and techniques that will consistently improve your writing.
- Develop the lifelong habits of a professional writer.

Available from your favorite online booksellers. Learn more at http://www.writingforward.com/books.

About the Author

Melissa Donovan is the founder and editor of *Writing Forward*, a blog packed with creative writing tips and ideas.

Melissa started writing poetry and song lyrics at age thirteen. Shortly thereafter, she began keeping a journal. She studied at Sonoma State University, earning a BA in English with a concentration in creative writing. Since then, Melissa has worked as an author, copywriter, professional blogger, and writing coach.

Writing Forward

Writing Forward features creative writing tips, ideas, tools, and techniques, as well as writing exercises and prompts that offer inspiration and help build skills.

To get more writing tips and ideas and to receive notifications when new books in the *Adventures in Writing* series are released, visit Writing Forward.

www.writingforward.com

29929223R00121

Made in the USA
Middletown, DE
08 March 2016